THE ROOT OF THE MATTER

THE ROOT OF THE MATTER

*A study in the connections between religion,
psychology and education*

by

MARGARET ISHERWOOD

with a foreword by
GERALD HEARD

GREENWOOD PRESS, PUBLISHERS
WESTPORT, CONNECTICUT

Copyright 1954 by Margaret Isherwood

Reprinted by permission
of Harper & Row, Publishers, New York

First Greenwood Reprinting 1970

Library of Congress Catalogue Card Number 79-90534

SBN 8371-3962-7

Printed in the United States of America

. . . Grant that I may grow to beauty in the things within, and that outward possessions may not disturb the harmony of the inner man. The wise man only may I consider rich; and of wealth may I have so much as only the wise man can bear.

Prayer of Socrates: *The Phaedrus*.

CONTENTS

ERRATA NOTICE

The sentence beginning on page 43, line 9 should read:
The Church obstructs growth process when it places the main emphasis on certain dubiously historical facts, and offers salvation through an unreflecting belief in these facts rather than through individual effort and adventurous search.

Page 27, line 4
Insert comma after word *content*.

Page 221, line 14
sun should appear *sunt*.

Page 225, line 10
amendable should appear *amenable*.

FOREWORD

OUR CHIEF NEED to-day is not more information, but co-ordination of the information we now possess. The most valuable books are then 'bridge' books—books that show the connection between divergent ways of thinking. The biggest of these divergencies is the chasm between science and religion. Science is unquestioned in its interpretation and management of the outer world, but it has not been able to be of anything like equal service in helping us to understand and to manage the inner world, the world of our consciousness.

Religion has always claimed and often demonstrated that this vast inner world is handled by the creative emotions, not by the critical intellect. But for the most part religion has said this in such odd language and asserted so many unsubstantiated things about the outer world, that science could not understand what it was driving at and was sure that many of its illustrations and arguments were untrue.

Miss Isherwood, with courageous knowledge of both sides, shows how the necessary bridge may be built. Religion, she points out, is the art of consciousness; science is the skill of power; and education the link between both. With her extensive knowledge of children and child psychology, she shows how, from the restorative successes that faith, hope and love have worked with the young, we may make a living and growing religion for ourselves. No theme can be more vital for us all. This is a book from which no reader could fail to gain personal help and encouragement as to our future.

GERALD HEARD.

9

PREFACE

I SHOULD LIKE TO make it clear that this book is not intended either for the orthodox believer or the orthodox atheist.

Those who find a satisfactory way of religious life within the Church, and can accept its doctrines literally, will not in any case be interested in it: and the dogmatic atheist who 'knows' there is no God and that life has no meaning beyond the 'here and now' also 'knows' that any attempt to suggest otherwise is nothing but a form of phantasy thinking.

It is for the uncertain and the seekers that the book is written; for those who, having lost their faith for one reason or another, have regretfully left the Church because they could not with integrity remain in it. Or for those who, while rejecting the doctrines of the Church, yet value its social and spiritual aspects and do not therefore altogether dissociate themselves from it, but feel somewhat confused and guilty because of their equivocal position. It is also for those who have never had a faith to lose, but who vaguely feel there is 'Something' to which they might subscribe if only they knew what it was. And, lastly, it is for those who feel pretty sure that life is meaningless and futile, but who are still open-minded enough to listen to an alternative possibility. The book is not an attack on the Church, but a challenge to it—a challenge that it should translate its doctrines, in so far as they have validity, into the language and modes of thought of the age; that it should enrich its teachings by the incorporation of all that is valid and relevant in modern psychology, particularly in the sphere of psycho-therapy and education (as once, after some resistance, it enriched itself by the incorporation of modern science). For it is becoming increasingly evident that many people to-day feel little or no interest in traditional religion and are more ready to turn to a psychologist than to a minister to help them discover some meaning to life, and to cope with the problems of living. The reason for this lies partly in the narrow theological training which produces clergy who, sighing over their empty pews, ask plaintively, 'But what can one do save put the Bible before people?'

Under the late Archbishop Temple, the Church of England made valiant efforts to embody the social teaching of Christianity; to see to it that men did get bread to eat and work to do. It is now time to stress the psychological and complementary fact that man does not live by bread alone, but that he has an equally basic hunger—the hunger for meaning. Doubtless the Church would reply that 'meaning' is exactly what it exists to provide, but the fact remains that for large numbers of seekers the indictment of Milton still holds: 'The hungry sheep look up and are not fed.'

M. Isherwood.

HOW TO AVOID THE BREAKDOWN OF
FAITH BY A CHANGE OF APPROACH

Twentieth-century man has lost a meaningful world, and a self
that lives in meanings out of a spiritual centre.

PAUL TILLICH.

THAT LOSS OF FAITH and break away from Church
authority is a characteristic mark of the age is obvious to any
observer, and is indeed frankly admitted by the Church
itself. No less an authority than the Archbishop of York
writes of this 'drift from religion': 'Everywhere, to a greater
or less degree, religious creeds and customs, whether
Christian or non-Christian, have suffered from the dis-
integrating effects of two world wars.' But, he adds, 'it
would be a mistake, however, to think the falling away from
religion is due solely, or even mainly, to the wars. They
hastened and brought to a head tendencies which had
already been undermining religious faith. If there had been
no wars, the Churches would have suffered both from open
hostility and from the far-reaching changes in the intellectual
atmosphere.'[1]*

The churches appear to be fuller in America, but among
the 'intellectuals' the record is the same. A recent research
into the religious life of the colleges shows that 56 per cent.
of the students have abandoned the Church of their upbringing. This would hardly be regarded as a satisfactory state
of affairs in any other department of life. Whitehead states
that 'Protestant Christianity . . . is showing all the signs of a

* For notes see p. 229.

13

steady decay. Its dogmas no longer dominate: its divisions no longer interest: its institutions no longer direct the patterns of life.'[2]

The following random collection of questions, comments, criticisms from peoples of all ages, illustrates the rudderless condition of the non-believer:

'What am I to teach my child?'

'You're going to church? Whatever for?'

'Oh, yes, I'm an agnostic myself, but I send the children to church in case they can find something there to help them through life.'

'Surely you don't believe in immortality? You can't possibly!'

'What on earth can one say to young people nowadays to make them feel that anything matters?'

'I think perhaps you are right that there is something other than orthodox religion, but what is it?'

'Religion is the blend of a sense of guilt and a sense of inferiority—nothing more.'

'I never felt the need of religion and I never met a child who did.'

'Don't tell me you're in danger of becoming a Christian.'

'What exactly *do* you believe?'

'Why does God allow it?'

'If one really believed that God created the world, it would be hard to forgive him.'

'Religion is a sentimental makeshift for love.'

'Religion is a need one should have outgrown.'

'I'd like to go to church, but I'm not going to stand up and say I believe in the Virgin Birth when I don't.'

The following remarks came from adolescents:

'God, from the scientific point of view, is an impossibility.'

'I want to make meaning out of life.'

'Look here, is there a God or isn't there?'

'How do you know it's not your subconscious seeking satisfaction in religious phantasy?'

'What is life all about? I mean what is it *for*? It doesn't make any sense.'

'Religion bores me.'

'I was brought up as a Churchman but when they said you must believe or be damned, I was through.'

And the following came from children of seven:

'Who made God?'

'You know I don't believe any of this.'

'Why do people go to church? It's such a stupid waste of time.'

'If God wanted people to be good, why didn't He make them good?'

'What are the causes of this widespread scepticism, revolt, and critical loss of faith? What are the 'undermining tendencies' to which the Archbishop refers? The main cause is the scientific temper of the age in which we live. 'Science shines out while religion is flickering,'[3] says Alexis Carrel. The attitude of 'if you want me to believe that, you must prove it' is both typical and inevitable. Now that the 'acid' of the scientific spirit has crumbled its foundations, authority is no longer regarded as a source of truth. Ever since Galileo insisted on the right to look through his telescope and discover for himself whether there were moons round Jupiter, rather than accept the authority of the Church on the matter, the enquiring mind has claimed a similar freedom, and rightly feels that both self-respect and the cause of truth demand it. The fearful man resists this venturesomeness and (like the medieval priest in the story), refuses to look through the telescope in case he should see the moons and have to adjust his thinking to this new evidence, or, worse still, perhaps lose his anchorage altogether in this precarious world. Better hold on to the authority which had served thus far: 'I have read Aristotle and the Bible,' said the prosecuting priest, 'and I find no reference there to moons round Jupiter.'

The modern expression of this drama of the struggle between the forces that hold back and the forces that adventure is, in the sphere of religion at any rate, less drastic and terrible than in the time of Galileo. But although the free-thinker is no longer victimised (indeed, it is sometimes the believer who is now at a disadvantage), yet the battle does go on in a more civilised form. A typical illustration of it is given by Sir Edward Marsh in his autobiography, where he writes that he had an extremely good and pious mother who spent many hours praying for her son's salvation and for his preservation from heretical views. At some financial sacrifice, she chose Cambridge for him rather than Oxford lest he should be contaminated by the High Church Movement at the latter. 'But the unlooked-for upshot was that I hadn't been a term at Trinity before I was caught by the prevailing tide of agnosticism, and every vestige of dogmatic belief fell away from me, never to return.'[4]

Similar wasteful, and sometimes injurious, breakdowns of faith will continue until both science and religion alike have enlarged their horizons and come to realise that there is no necessary antagonism between them because they are concerned with different realms of experience, involving different modes of approach to truth. And in so far as both are concerned with the search for truth, there should be no quarrel between them. But so long as religion is primarily conceived as dogma to be believed rather than as reverence for life, and so long as science remains sure that reason alone can reveal truth, the deadlock will continue.

A second main cause of the prevailing scepticism and loss of interest in religion lies in the failure of the Church to keep abreast of the psychological thought of the age, particularly in the sphere of educational and of child psychology. This failure can be seen in various ways. For example, little attempt is made to see that there is a correspondence between what is taught and what goes on in the mind of the child. In her *Search for a Soul*, Phyllis Bottome describes her desperate effort to come to terms with religion and to find out what it was all about:

'I knew there was something in it which was probably

truer than anything else, but strive as I might, I broke my teeth against it in all the various forms it was presented to me. I loved the Gospel stories but no one I knew behaved the least like Christ. I enjoyed Church services; but I saw no connection whatever between them and anybody else's daily life. . . .'[5]

This statement illustrates not only the failure of the religious educationalist to enter into the mind of the child, but the failure to face up to the gulf which exposes the Church to the charge of hypocrisy—the gulf which exists between Christian teaching and practice, between such precepts as 'Love your enemies' or 'Sell all that you have and give to the poor' and the fact that many Christian pastors and masters would think you a fool if you tried to do the first and heartily disapprove if you did the second. Or the still more perplexing gulf that seems to be inherent in Christ's teaching on the nature of reality, between 'Be not anxious for your Father knoweth that ye have need of all these things,' and the facts of poverty, misery, earthquake, famine, fire and flood; or between 'If ye shall ask anything in My name I will do it,' and the fact of unanswered prayer.

Christ's absolute directives such as 'resist not evil' or 'Be ye perfect' should be understood to refer to the ultimate goal towards which we strive. Taken literally, they tend to induce scepticism or despair. The boy Stephen believed the absolute statement that he had been taught in Sunday school, 'Everyone that asketh receiveth,' and so he prayed with desperate urgency that God would spare the life of his sick father. His father died and an atheist was born. The woman who had been told in chapel that God is Love made the logical response when her beloved husband was crushed to death in the mine: 'If I set foot in chapel again, it will be in my box and knowing nothing of it.'[6] And Silas Marner, after the cruel vestry trial that destroyed him, cried out in the torment of his misery: 'There is no just God that judges the earth righteously.'

The persistence of faith under such circumstances would

sometimes seem more surprising than the loss of it. At any rate, there is a strong psychological case for not giving children a religion of absolutes and certainties which life may later fail to substantiate. Martha's mother was not very helpful when her five-year-old asked suddenly, 'Do you believe in God?' but at least she was not evasive, hypocritical or authoritarian as she replied, 'No, I don't; but a lot of people do, and you can if you want to.' Since there was no emotional compulsion either way, the child felt free to reply, after a moment's reflection: 'Yes, I think I'd like to.' She was better off than Stephen and Silas and the miner's widow with their simple absolutes that did not stand the test of experience, because she received at least a glimmering of the idea that each must explore the truth about God for himself, and that partial knowledge is all that we should hope for and all that we can in the nature of things achieve. The same applies to the young theologian Judy, who, sitting on her father's knee, asked in surprise, 'Why can't you answer my question, Daddy?' She received the doubtless unsatisfactory response, 'Because, Judy, there are so many things I do not know.' But she also received things more valuable than any verbal information: a sense of her father's integrity and of his respect for her as an individual who should not be silenced with trite and superficial answers; she received the warmth of his affectionate understanding and the joy of sharing with him the beauty of the sunset they were watching together. It may also be that, because of these things, she received a hint of that

'sense sublime of something far more deeply interfused, Whose dwelling is the light of setting suns.'

One thing we can opine: she would be unlikely to suffer from loss of faith so long as her religious life continued to be built on such inner experiences of her relatedness to love and beauty rather than on lofty precepts bearing no relation to life because impossible of achievement.

18

Another defect in the psychology of religious education is the failure to observe stages of development and to adapt the teaching accordingly. In the East it was long ago recognised that a growing mind must inevitably think differently and entertain different concepts of God as different steps in the approach to religious maturity. The religion of a mature man ought not to be the same as that of a child, as St. Paul himself pointed out.

In the biography already referred to, the following incident is related: 'Mrs. Earle and her husband, both agnostics, were much exercised as to the attitude towards religion which they should take up in the education of their three little sons; so they laid their doubts before their friend, the great Huxley, and were set at ease by his well-weighed pronouncement: "My dear Mrs. Earle, you should bring the boys up in the mythology of their age and country." '[7]

The advice was sound so far as it went, but it was woefully inadequate. The probability is that sooner or later intelligent children will question this mythology when they start to think for themselves. Therefore, unless these boys had the good fortune to be educated by a man of insight, who not only knew how to adapt his teaching to their level of understanding, but who also recognised the necessity of helping them find new meanings and deeper interpretations in the old forms, and of tracing with them the underlying truths common to all great religious traditions, then the chances were that the baby would go out with the bath-water once again in spite of Huxley's 'well-weighed pronouncement'. It is true that there are quite good reasons for bringing up children in 'the mythology of their age and country,' but what Huxley omitted to give his friends was some advice on the transitional periods, more especially on the daring and enquiring stage of adolescence (when a Child of twelve once presumed to question the Doctors in the Temple).

A further defect in the psychology of religious education has been the tendency of ecclesiastical authority to frown upon this doubting and exploring tendency, and offer it no alternative to 'Believe or . . .' 'She says she doesn't believe,' complained thirteen-year-old Mary's priest to her mother. 'It is no use sending her to me for instruction. I can't do anything with a person who doesn't believe.' That is true. He would have done better to take instruction himself in some elementary educational psychology, and to have asked himself whether commending a person to believe what they find no adequate grounds for believing does not savour of intellectual dishonesty.

In addition to the failure to recognise specific stages of development, still another failure has been to ignore psychological differences of temperament. Here again the wisdom of the East has exceeded our wisdom, for it long ago recognised that there are varieties of psychological and spiritual temperament, and on the strength of this discovery it differentiated four or five approaches to truth or to union with God, each one of which was to be used, not exclusively, but predominantly, by the individual according to his temperamental type.

It is customary for Western man to dismiss with a sneer these yogas or modes of union, but that sneer is the measure of our ignorance. In view of the state of Western civilisation, a little humility and willingness to learn from others would be more becoming. And since secular education does now make some attempt to fit square pegs into square holes and to let each individual develop in accordance with his psychophysical constitution, it should not be too difficult to extend the same idea to the religious life, and to allow each to arrive at the spiritual truth (knowledge of God), of which he is capable in his own way as well as in his own time: some primarily through action (*Karma yoga*); some by intellectual knowledge (*Jnana*); some by knowledge gained through working on experience (*Rajah*), and some by personal devotion (*Bhakti*—perhaps the predominantly Christian type). No one way should exclude the rest; and since all are valid, there is no place for intolerance of the contemplative by the activist, of the student by the artist, of the thinking by the feeling type or vice versa.

We have achieved a similar tolerance in 'secular' education, but there is still much intolerance in religious circles. 'It sounds High Church. Beware,' said a mother to her daughter entering college. She should have said, 'Be interested.' The important thing is not merely to emphasise the right to differences of approach, but to recognise that religion is a way; not an absolute truth once and for all delivered and automatically yours if you will only believe it; but a path to be followed with much striving, a path of inner growth which will ultimately bring just that degree of knowledge that inner achievement has made possible. This view of religion is psychologically more sound than the view that stresses primarily right doctrine and the duty of the individual to believe what authority teaches. It is less likely to break down through unbelief; it will involve no wasteful unlearning, no injurious suffering as a result of loss of faith, and no feeling of having been tricked, with consequent resentment against a Church that 'misled' it.

And this points to the last of the main causes of breakdown in Western religion—a cause which is partly psychological, partly moral: exclusiveness. Not only is there intolerance between the different branches of the Christian Church for each other; there is not, for the main part, any serious attempt to study with interest and lack of prejudice the non-Christian religions. A closed mind is not a desirable or courageous attitude, and the fact that some apostates from the Christian Church have been able to find what they sought in these non-Christian fields should discourage the negative attitude of exclusiveness among the leaders of the Christian Churches and cause them to enquire, without prejudice, whether other religions may have something they have missed. To see non-Christian religions merely as fields for proselytising rather than for interested exploration indicates an egocentricity which is none the less harmful for being mainly unconscious.

The following case illustrates this transference of allegiance and gives at least some of the reasons for it:

'Soon after my confirmation I began to discover that I had, as they say, "lost my faith"; or, to be more exact, I discovered that I had never had any. By the time I was twenty, I declared myself an atheist, and I remained in that conviction for the next fifteen years. I said, publicly and privately, that I loathed religion; that it was evil, superstitious, reactionary nonsense, and I warmly agreed that it was indeed "the opium of the people". These statements were taken as a matter of course by my friends, who were, with one or two exceptions, all of the same opinion as myself.' The writer continues: 'By religion I meant the Christian religion or, more specifically, the Church of England, into which I had been received by baptism when I was a baby; other Christian sects I had been encouraged to suspect or despise: the Catholics were traditionally "un-English" and involved in sinister international politics; the Nonconformists were common and lower middle class. as for the Hindus, Buddhists and Mohammedans, they were merely picturesque heathens who wailed from minarets, spun prayer wheels, and flung themselves under juggernauts. You couldn't count on them as being "religious" at all. Such were the attitudes I inherited . . . and, one might add, they were and are common enough attitudes in much Protestant upbringing.'[8]

This author ultimately found in Vedanta a religious approach which appealed to him. 'Previously,' he says, 'I had always thought of religion in terms of dogmas, commandments and declarative statements. The teacher expounded the truth, the dogmatic ultimatum; you, the pupil, had only to accept it in its entirety. Your sole alternative was to reject it altogether. But Vedanta made me understand for the first time that a practical working religion is experimental and empirical. You are always on your own, finding out things for yourself in your individual way. Vedanta starts off with a single proposition which is no more than a working hypothesis: "The Atman can be known." '

Obviously this is not the approach for everyone; neither is it suggested, in spite of Vivekananda (who said, 'It is a tragedy not to be born into a Church, but it is a tragedy to die in one'), that it is necessary to leave the Church of one's upbringing. The majority of minds need a certain 'concreteness' in the framework of their faith. But it is necessary that growth should continuously take place within that framework, it is necessary that the emphasis should be laid on the path rather than on the person, and it is necessary that the truth in other frameworks should not be ignored or belittled.

Having discussed the causes, let us look next at some of the consequences of loss of faith. These naturally vary with the temperament and circumstances of the individual. Some can shed their beliefs as lightly as they would shed an old coat; for others the process may be long drawn out over the years and very devastating. This is especially likely to be the case where a child has not been able to build good and stable emotional relationships in early life, and consequently uses religion as a substitute for a broken or unhappy home. The Father in Heaven gives the security that the earthly parents, for one reason or another, fail to provide. As the Psalmist puts it: 'When my father and mother forsake me the Lord taketh me up.' Many a child and many an adult has been enabled to bear over-heavy burdens in this reliance. If, therefore, faith in God the Father is challenged and undermined before a sufficiently strong ego-structure has been built up, and before that faith has been re-stated and comprehended as faith in God the Spirit (which cannot be undermined because it is experienced), then the individual is twice bereft, and may not have the strength to face his loss.

The intimacy of this connection between the individual's emotional dependency and his religion is illustrated in recent studies into the effect of the loss of their moorings on young children. In her book *Infants Without Families*, an account of wartime evacuees, Anna Freud describes what

23

happened to infants who were constantly being moved from one foster-parent or mother-substitute to another. It was always injurious, and in some cases the child ended by losing the capacity for further adaptation and became apathetic and lifeless. It was as if he said to himself, 'Why form yet another love relationship only to face the pain of loss and deprivation all over again?'

The psychological mechanism in such cases is exactly the same as that involved in loss of belief in God, and it is not surprising that those who have lived through it should advocate a purely humanistic education. Priscilla Robertson, in a recent article, makes a very strong case against teaching any religious dogma to the young, largely because of her own father's experience. He was the son of a minister and 'was brought up so piously that his first serious idea of a career was to become a minister himself, possibly a missionary. In college, however (partly from reading Gibbon), he came to believe that the God he wished to serve didn't exist. The discovery was so painful to him that he resolved to spare any child of his a similar struggle.'[9] This shattering experience, known in psychological parlance as 'trauma', which often results from loss of faith, is described by another college graduate as follows:

'After the first impact of the shock, I felt as if the ground was literally giving way beneath my feet. My life was centred on and supported by God, and if after all no God was there, then I was bereft indeed. At night I wandered despairingly under the stars beseeching Him for a sign that He did exist; in the daytime I went back and forth from my religious friends, who prayed for my return to the fold, to my agnostic friends, who rejoiced in my emancipation and would have had scant respect for a recidivist. For years I wandered miserably in a great fog, refusing the way of credulity, yet hating the way of unbelief. Finally, in later life, a path began to emerge out of the darkness, a path which I might have seen much sooner had not my early conditioning caused me to look for the wrong kind of answers and to expect more specific knowledge about the nature of God and the Universe than is permitted to mortal man in his present stage of development.'

How seriously traumatic this early loss of faith can be is a matter needing fuller attention. Adolescence is always an emotionally unstable period. If, during this period, the individual's main support and fulcrum is his religion, then the sudden demolition of that religion may be as devastating an experience as a major disappointment in love, and, like the latter, may lead to serious depression and breakdown. Proal has noted that a proportion of the suicides among adolescents is due to precocious scepticism. 'Suicide is the natural and logical termination for a being in whom has been destroyed the interest which was the motive power of life.'[10] Even where the consequence is not so drastic as suicide, the individual is often left with a sense of the futility and meaninglessness of life. He may also, if poorly endowed with a natural feeling for virtue, be left with an indifference to character and conduct that has serious consequences for the whole of society, for, if one's moral code has been related to and directed by the Church, the chances are that morality will be considerably weakened if and when the Church loses its authority. Consciously or unconsciously, the argument would run: 'I was told not to do this or that because God would disapprove; now that I don't believe in God, I can do what I please.'

Thus develops that 'ugly chaos' to which Beatrice Webb feelingly referred when she wrote some twenty years ago: 'Like so many of my contemporaries, I am a religious outcast. I cannot enjoy, without sacrificing intellectual integrity, the immeasurable benefit of spiritual companionship, the inner peace, arising out of traditional forms of worship, the inspiration of noble motive—all of which I recognise as embodied in the great religions of the world, such as Christianity and Buddhism. And while I rejoice in the advance of science, I deplore the desuetude of regular religious services with the encouragement and prayer, for the good reason that personal experience and the study of history convince me that this absence of the religious habit leads to an ugly chaos in private and public morals, and to a subtle lowering of the sense of duty. Witness the idol of the sub-human and the prevalence of crude animalism, in much of the music, literature and art of the twentieth century.'[11]

We are, therefore, impelled to the conclusion that the individual's conscience is best built in free and friendly relationship with others on a non-authoritarian basis. A recent *Church Times* review of *Martin Merridew*, by Mary Borden, stated: 'This novel strips naked the fanatic who thinks that a private revelation of religion is better than the faith of the Church; and it shows the hell into which a soul may enter when the anchor of belief has slipped.' The fact that the hero of the book comes to disaster and shame in his unbelief is used as an argument for sticking close to Mother Church, but it might be more pertinently used as an argument for urging Mother Church to help her children achieve a spiritual maturity based on something less precarious than her own authoritative doctrines.

What that 'something' might be, the rest of this book is an attempt to explore, but to the father who asked helplessly, 'What am I to teach my child?' we can at least say this: 'You can only teach what you yourself have found.' Words will be but tinkling cymbals unless they come out of genuine personal experience, and unless they correspond to the way of life of the speaker. Religious education must take place primarily through religious being, and if the gap between precept and practice is too obvious, the child can only reply in effect: 'What you are speaks so loudly that I cannot hear what you say.' Words, of course, have a useful function in passing on the wisdom of the tradition, but we can no more teach religion than we can teach beauty or love or joy by words alone.

In the last resort, there is no distinction between sacred and secular, and all education is, or should be, religious. Whether or not we share Professor Dewey's desire to emancipate the religious from religion, to dispense with the noun and keep only the adjective, we must at least agree that religious education is primarily a matter of attitude rather than of doctrinal content of the spirit in which teaching is conducted rather than what is taught, and that its emphasis should be on example rather than precept; on imaginative understanding rather than rote learning; on free discussion rather than imposed utterances; on delight in knowledge rather than on a concern with its utility; on good feeling rather than on correct behaviour; on insight into meaning rather than lip service to orthodoxy; on ordered freedom rather than on order or freedom alone. But these are the characteristics of all true education, and in so far as any education embodies them it is to that extent religious. Whether the subject be mathematics, history, biology or the Scriptures, the teacher whose delight it is to awaken a sense of wonder at the beauty and relatedness of his subject, and so further the all-round spiritual, intellectual and emotional development of his pupils, is, to that extent, a religious teacher. Head, heart and hand; thought, feeling and doing; imagination, appreciation and activity must all be harmoniously operative if the child's faith in life is to be so securely based that it cannot break down.

CHAPTER I

FROM THE THEOLOGICAL APPROACH
TO THE PSYCHOLOGICAL

I've studied now Philosophy
And Jurisprudence, Medicine,
And even, alas, Theology,
With vision keen, from end to end.
And yet, poor fool, with all my lore
I am no wiser than before.

GOETHE.

AND SO DR. FAUST was unable to find the meaning of
life in books, not even, 'alas', in theological ones. He does
not mention psychology. Could he perchance have found
there the answer that he was seeking? And can modern
man find, in a study of himself, the meaning that he cannot
find either in theology or in the external world?

The very suggestion must fill both the orthodox and the
hearty extravert with horror and perhaps not without good
reason. And yet there is that difficult psychological assertion:
'The Kingdom of Heaven is within you.' What 'on earth'
did Christ mean? Of late years modern psychology has been
very busy looking within, but what it has found would
hardly appear to coincide with the average person's idea of
the Kingdom of Heaven.

During the last war, Dorothy Sayers once wrote that
'Unless the post-war world begins by understanding what
sort of creature man is, it has no hope of accomplishing
anything.' What sort of creature does analytic psychology
reveal man to be? What does it say about the nature of
human nature?

At first glance, its report would not appear to be start-

28

lingly different from that of the theologians and the Old Testament prophets. Granted that the psychologist has a different approach and a different attitude towards his findings from that of the theologian, because his business is to portray rather than to reform, to avoid judgemental terms like 'sin' and, as a scientist, to indulge no moralistic approval or disapproval; yet there is basic similarity in what is revealed, and the average man might well wonder whether it is any more helpful to be told by Freud that we are 'ravening wolves' than to be told by the Psalmist that we are born in sin; to learn from Jung that we are driven by a dark 'Shadow' in the unconscious, or to learn from David that the heart of man is deceitful above all things and desperately wicked. Human nature looks like a bad business either way, whether as presented by the scientist or by the moralist. Of course, psychology, like religion, recognises the 'good' in man as well as the 'evil'. It goes to the extremes neither of Calvin on the one hand nor of Rousseau on the other, in refusing to look at the entire picture. The question is: Has it an answer as to what should be done to diminish the tension between these opposing forces by strengthening the good? 'Part of him really wanted to go straight, but another part of him was stronger,' said the probation officer of his delinquent ward, repeating in twentieth-century terms the ancient cry of St. Paul: 'The good that I would, I do not: the evil that I would not, that I do.' And if psychology cannot prevent or diminish the tension, can it cure breakdowns that result when the tensions can no longer be endured—breakdowns into delinquency or neurosis or both?

Again, at first glance, it might seem questionable. But in this sphere it is impossible to make definite and accurate estimates. Psychotherapeutic factors cannot be entirely separated from other influences which may be equally potent, and in any case, who is to estimate what constitutes a permanently successful 'cure'? However, the following statements on the negative side are here given for what they are worth.

In a book called *The Case against Psycho-analysis*, Andrew Salter describes an extensive study of mental patients with whom analysis is said to have failed somewhat more often than it succeeded. In *The Devils of Loudun*, Aldous Huxley quotes a psychologist who, having made careful study of the matter, finds 'that in mental disorders the proportion of cures has remained, for nearly two hundred years, remarkably constant, whatever the nature of the psychiatric methods employed. The percentage of cures claimed by modern psycho-analysts is no higher than the percentage of cures claimed by the alienists of 1800.[1] And, thirdly, there are numbers of mainly subjective reports from therapists and their associates who would not claim to have made any careful statistical check-up, but whose observations deserve attention. One such observer writes: 'My experience as a layman who has for a long time been on the fringes of the mental illness field has gradually brought me to the conclusion that not more than a small percentage permanently recover due to psychotherapeutic treatment. There may be a high percentage of temporary recovery, but in the long run those who once yield to their emotional conflicts have a tendency to slip back from time to time when the pressure gets rough again. After all, the kind of world we live in must produce much of the psychoneurotic and psychotic difficulties these days. When the purpose of psychotherapy is to adjust people to the sort of world that unadjusts them, we can see the dilemma confronting psychotherapists and patients alike. Even the therapists themselves cannot escape this problem of personal adjustment to this sort of a world, and anyone with wide experience knows how often we see the therapist himself slip into the emotional swamp from which he is trying to extricate his patient. This long-run ineffectiveness of psychotherapy may be only a temporary phase, for it is only in its infancy, and with new knowledge and with continual experimentation, the day may soon come when it can take its place alongside other areas of medical science which produce high rates of healing.'

If that were all that modern psychology and psychotherapy could show to its credit, we might be pardoned for not feeling very much confidence in it and the Church might well feel justified in ignoring it. But it is not all. Psychology has made some very definite and important contributions to our knowledge of human nature and of its mode of functioning. The results of its discoveries are not measurable and not yet fully understood, but they will eventually spread far beyond the confines of the clinic, and will, if used in collaboration with religious and educational knowledge, enable us to make real progress. Is it a small thing, for example, to have learnt how little we know about our deep selves, and that the most powerful motivations in our lives are often hidden, not only from others, but from ourselves; that we build up a very respectable façade or *persona* to present to the world and let down the portcullis on the rest, fondly imagining that we have thereby disposed of it; that without knowing it, we project the unacceptable with which we have not been able to come to terms in ourselves, and then condemn it comfortably and without embarrassment in others; that we also project our emotional needs on to others, making them into our mothers, fathers, children, thus using them as means to serve our ends rather than treating them as ends in themselves?

In the seventeenth century these things were unknown, and it was therefore possible for his enemies in the Church to torture and burn Father Urbain Grandier as a sorcerer because they questioned neither their own motives nor those of Sœur Jeanne, who accused him. And since the unconscious part of man's mind listens gladly to accusations against its enemies, the rejected nun was easily able to carry through her terrible revenge on the priest who had ignored her importunities.

In the same century, it was also possible for a great and pious Church dignitary, Père Josef, to set Europe aflame in the Thirty Years' War and believe he was doing God's service because, although he had techniques for inducing mystical

31

experience, he had none for getting into touch with his real motives, and was totally unaware of the hidden lust for power in himself, which was masquerading as piety. A similar example of this 'blissful' unawareness was given at an earlier date by Bishop Cauchon, who at the trial of Joan gave in all 'sincerity' a most convincing case as to why she must be condemned if she would not accept the authority of the Church as primary.

These examples from history are not intended to suggest that such things no longer happen. Persecutions to-day are just as terrible as in the seventeenth century. In the sphere of the new secular totalitarian 'religions', all sorts of horrors are being perpetrated from motives of power lust dolled up as love of humanity. Ignorance of the real nature of our drives is still the rule rather than the exception. But we no longer have the same excuse for refusing to look at the unconscious mechanisms that control us, for the dynamics of self-delusion and unconscious hypocrisy are clearly described in the text-books for any who wish to study them. To detect these mechanisms at work in ourselves is, of course, a very much more difficult task than reading about them, but everyone can make a start if he will.

Another psychological contribution of quite enormous and far-reaching importance has already become common knowledge to the average reader—namely, that much neurotic illness and moral delinquency has its origin in the emotional experiences of early life. This discovery has been arrived at from opposite ends of the tunnel, so to speak. The depth psychologist unearths in the grown man memories of early infancy which are powerfully operative in his adult life; and the child psychologist observes the infant itself, and notes the devastating effect on him, of the deprivation of mother love or of other emotional loss, especially during the first twelve months in his life.

From these observations we learn that while it is good for the social conscience to see to it that children are adequately clothed and fed and do not suffer from vitamin deficiency, there is the possibility of a deficiency in the emotional life which free milk and physical care can do nothing to redress. Facts such as those disclosed by John Bowlby in *Child Care and the Growth of Love* should give much food for thought to legislators of any party who fondly imagine that all life's problems can be solved by the creation of a just social system, by the provision of good food and housing for all. And ministers of all creeds will find in this book at least one of the reasons why, in spite of age-long preaching, people find such difficulty in obeying Christ's second commandment; why, instead of freely loving each other, individuals may withdraw from life, become incapable of giving or receiving affection and sink into depression and emotional atrophy. Or why, on the other hand, they may become filled with hatred and desire for revenge, or make excessive demands for privileges which will compensate them for the deprivation of love, and perhaps end up in delinquency when these privileges are not forthcoming; or will try to buy affection with material gifts, sometimes secured with stolen money.

Let it not be inferred that all human problems are traceable to any one cause, such as deprivation of love in infancy, or that wisely loving parents will automatically and inevitably have good children. Life is a good deal more complex than that. But what a wisely loving home can do is to make goodness a little less difficult, and mental and moral illness a little less easy. And what we are here concerned to emphasise is the immense importance of this particular discovery of the absolute necessity of mother love in infancy to the emotional health of the child. For, so far as religion is concerned, it should be clear that no healthy religion can be built on an unhealthy emotional life; therefore a minister cannot be called 'trained' who does not know his psychology as well as his theology. And so far as society is concerned, it is, viewed even from the lowest standpoint of utility, less costly to put some form of protection at the top of the cliff to prevent malfunctioning than an ambulance to receive the casualties at the bottom. (It should be noted in passing that the word 'psychology' now covers so much variety of ground that it is too general to be useful without further specification. As used in this book, it refers primarily to the spheres of child psychology and psychotherapy, for these are the aspects of the subject that relate to religion and religious education.)

It is sad, therefore, to find the Archbishop of York in his recent book, *In an Age of Revolution*, giving so little attention to what is surely the greatest revolution of our day; such scant recognition of what psychology can achieve and such disproportionate emphasis on its negative aspects. The Archbishop expresses a fear that psychology can be used as a dangerous weapon against religion. In so far as that may be true, it is as nothing compared with the immense support psychology can be to religion when both are concerned with the search for truth rather than with the propagation of 'my' truth.

Dr. Garbett admits that 'the psycho-analyst can often give valuable help in restoring a divided personality and in removing irrational phobias; but,' he adds, 'the tendency of much psychological teaching is to blunt the difference between right and wrong. . . . Psychology is often taught and understood as if it gave a satisfactory explanation of religion and a valid reason for not worrying about sin.'[2]

There is, of course, truth in this indictment. Let us frankly admit that some psychologists are so mechanistic in outlook as to convey the impression that they believe all behaviour is causally determined: and that there is therefore no place for individual responsibility. (Whether they do in fact really believe this is questionable, since they do not hesitate to exercise moral judgement and use the word 'ought' when the occasion calls for it.) But admittedly, the consequences of their teaching can be deplorable. For example, a brilliant young student who felt that her desires ought to be gratified was in the habit of helping herself to other people's possessions. When caught in the act,

34

she blandly remarked with Erewhonian detachment: 'Perhaps I ought to be psycho-analysed.' (There is of course such a thing as pathological stealing, not uncommon among children, for which psychotherapy is to be recommended; but such was not the case here.)

This irresponsible attitude of handing over to society and of refusing to undertake the burdensome task of one's own character growth is also frequently to be observed in the self-centred neurotic, bogged down in his own self-pity and self-protection. Having learnt, perhaps correctly, that all his troubles are due to an insufficiency of love and understanding in early life, he seizes on this interesting fact and clings to it as an excuse for making no further effort either to pull his own weight in the world or to transcend and find alternative satisfaction for his unsatisfied emotional needs. The self-excuser expresses himself in such statements as: 'You don't understand.' 'I never had a chance.' 'You can't expect anything from me after such a raw deal.' 'My father was jealous of me, my mother never really loved me, so I couldn't get to first base.' 'I was beaten at the start.'

Qui s'excuse s'accuse. The coward (and there is one in all of us) will snatch at anything, even modern psychology, and use it to justify his negativism, his self-pity and his moral indolence. When reminded that others too have suffered and have 'turned their necessity to glorious gain', he clings to his 'alibi' that no one ever suffered such deprivations as his; that others who were badly neglected in childhood, such as Comenius and Froebel, and yet used their suffering as a source of strength, must have had some advantages that he missed.

On such a craven attitude Christ long ago pronounced the relentless judgement: 'Thou wicked and unprofitable servant.' And if that sounds harsh to modern ears, let it be realised that the New Testament parable merely depicts, accurately, the way life is. Quite apart from the terrible verdict of the returning householder, life metes out its own verdict: 'those who break the law destroy themselves'.

35

The law is that we go forward courageously with what we have, however little that may be. If we do well with that little, we make it possible for ourselves to receive more, but if we refuse to co-operate with our negligible 'talent' it will be taken away from us—that is to say, it will inevitably atrophy from lack of use. In effect, life says to us: 'You are not required to achieve the same standard as others more richly endowed; you are required to do your utmost with what you have, without regrets and without complaints.'

But while admitting and deploring the type of psychologist who may have fostered such negative attitudes, we should in fairness also admit that it is not the most prevalent type. We do not judge medicine by its poorest practitioners. Why do so with psychology? Moreover, far from using psychology as a weapon against religion, no less a psychologist than Carl Jung has clearly stated that in a large number of mental patients, faith in life is a condition of recovery; that a merely reductive analysis which clears the ground and lays bare the dynamics of a neurosis is not enough; that it is of no use having the house of the soul swept and garnished if the individual feels no desire to go on living in it because he finds life loveless and meaningless. Such a despairing one says in effect: 'All right. I now realise that I am as I am because I was an unwanted child, or because I was insufficiently fed at the breast, or because I was frustrated and frightened in infancy. So what do I do about it? I don't feel any better just as a result of knowing these things; the emptiness is still there even though I now know what caused it. My capacity for loving was impaired and it remains impaired.' 'How often,' writes Jung, 'have I heard a patient exclaim: "If only I knew my life had some meaning and purpose, then there would be no silly story about my nerves." '[3] And again, in a passage that cannot be quoted too often, he tells us: 'Among all my patients in the second half of life—that is to say, over thirty-five—there has not been one whose problem in the last resort was not that of finding a religious outlook on life. It is safe to say that every one of them fell ill because he had lost that which the living religions of every age have given to their followers, and none of them has been really healed who did not regain his religious outlook. This, of course, has nothing whatever to do with a particular creed or membership of a Church.'[4] That is to say, regaining a religious outlook is not the same thing as regaining religious beliefs. No one should be persuaded to go back and try again to believe the theology he once believed; but rather to go forward into a new venture of faith in the meaningfulness of life, by seeking out truth for himself, by creating beauty, and by trying to serve others in love.

How to get this spiritual growth started in a sick mind, how to persuade the soil to receive the seed of God and foster it so that it does not die from inanition after it has been planted is the major problem in psychotherapy. The lack of a genuine desire to grow and change is the first obstacle, but even if that is overcome, nothing further can happen if the patient, as is so often the case, expects the therapist to do all the work for him in the fond delusion that 'treatment' is as passive a process as massage; that he can be 'made over' by some magic which makes no demands on him. Very different is the truth. The curative force is not just the willingness to receive the seed of new life, but to co-operate with it in courage and humility, to care for the soil and see to it that the ground is neither too shallow nor too choked with thistles for the seed to take root. In other words, to determine to come to grips with life and with his true self, and to endeavour to remove all obstacles that hinder the finding of the Kingdom within.

Therefore psychology, when followed through far enough, brings us to religion, or, rather, to religious experience in the form of rebirth of the spirit, of willingness to enter into new life and to use all that happens to us as a means of fostering that life. It is doubtful whether it could be generated in a patient save by one who knew in his own experience the meaning of being 'born again', and that is why Dr. Paul

37

Tillich says: 'Only a priestly man can be a complete psychologist.'[5]

So whether or not religion feels it can do without psychology, it is becoming steadily clearer that psychotherapy cannot do without religion—religion, that is, in its inward sense, as taught by Christ. Those who criticise psychology as the potential enemy of religion probably have in mind such a challenge as that of Freud in *The Nature of an Illusion*.

What Freud attacked however was not religious experience as such, but the dressing up of regressive emotional states in the garments of Church dogma and calling them religious; using orthodoxy as an excuse for avoiding the effort of growing up and of thinking for oneself. In *The Ego and the Id*, he says that both what is lowest and what is highest in the ego can be unconscious, and he believed that the natural aim of man's development should be towards the highest, towards virtue, and that a man who does not live a good life will become a sick man.

From this it follows that neither did Freud, as is again commonly supposed, advocate licence or the free and unrestrained expression of instinctive impulse. On the contrary, he explicitly states that civilisation is built upon the control of these impulses. The confusion has arisen over his unfortunate use of the word 'repression'. To the ordinary individual, repression means pretty much the same as restraint or control, but Freud took the word and gave it the specific connotation of 'unconscious forgetting', an extremely dangerous mental mechanism because it leads to a divided mind. What Freud wanted was that the instinctive life should be taken care of, controlled and sublimated with *conscious* intent. It is unawareness he deprecated, not self-control. Were this understood, one cause of the antagonism between religion and psychology would be removed.

Psychology then, in its aspect of therapy, is seen to be what it always has been in the East, the handmaid, not the alternative to religion. It cannot give meaning to life, but it can help to unfold life's meaning, by deepening one's understanding of the laws of growth and integrity, by demonstrating that these laws have their sanction in the nature of things, and cannot be broken with impunity. As one student put it: 'Psychology helps you to clarify your needs and ends by making you realise your deepest need is religious.' Psychology cannot, alone, rescue and re-create an individual, but it can help forward the process whereby such re-creation may become possible. For that matter, no one thing *alone* can save man, for the simple reason that

> 'All things by immortal power
> Near or far,
> Hiddenly
> To each other linkèd are.'[6]

The piecemeal approach to salvation has been tried many times in many spheres, and inevitably without success. The advocates of religion, politics, education, sociology, economics and psychology have each in turn been sure that with them alone lay the answer to life's problems. The political zealot of to-day is as sure that man can live by bread alone as religious zealots have sometimes been sure he could live without bread. The reformers in education have generally 'known' that education had all the keys. *'Education peut tout'* announced Helvetius. But it cannot, for the reasons given: all life is organically related and therefore all must be included. The arrogance of the over-simplifier who claims that heredity only or environment only is responsible for any effect, received its death-blow from the late Dr. Temple who, when informed by a youthful critic, 'You only believe what you believe because of your upbringing,' replied with unerring logic: 'And you only believe that I believe what I believe because of my upbringing, because of your upbringing.'

We are then compelled to admit the mutual need and interdependence of religion and psychology, for the first without the second is like medicine without research, and

39

will make no appeal to the modern seeker: and the second without the first is becalmed, like a sailing boat without wind. An impressive statement of this condition is given by Dr. Anton Boisen, Research Associate in the Psychology of Religion and Chaplain of the Elgin State Hospital. He writes: 'I can only say that, from the standpoint of the mentally ill in whose behalf I speak, I scarcely know which is worse; to have to depend on a clergyman who has never come to close grips with the realities of human nature, or to be at the mercy of a physician who has no understanding of the spiritual needs and aspirations and of the nobler potentialities of mankind.'[7] This does not mean that together psychology and religion can bring in the millennium, or even necessarily always effect a cure. Christ Himself had His failures, and, as we have seen, the patient must do his part. Without his determined goodwill as a growing point, neither the techniques of the therapist nor the prayers of the religionist will avail anything. But the chances of reorientation towards wholeness are greater if both work together, as is happening in the Pastoral Psychology Movement both in England and America.

A final reason for their co-operation lies in the cosmology of the age, with which theology must surely try to keep pace. More than once theology has ultimately had to abandon a good deal of fundamentalism and to assimilate new scientific discoveries, first of Copernican astronomy and later of the theory of evolution. It was not easy, because medieval theology gave men that security which they prize so highly. Fear of Hell was doubtless the most potent and most prevalent motive for being good, but at least you knew exactly what you had to do to escape eternal punishment. The cosmology of the time was clear-cut and static and gave people a definite and an apparently satisfactory and understandable idea of where they were—on a flat immobile earth (supported, in Chinese imagery, by four men standing on a turtle). It also gave specific information about the nature, locality and occupations of Heaven and Hell, and how to behave here if you wanted happiness hereafter. You could not go wrong save by deliberate heresy.

To-day physics presents a very different picture of the Universe—a Universe which Sir James Jeans describes as consisting of waves, 'Nothing but waves'. Matter, which appears to our senses as inert, heavy and 'dead', is in reality a form of force, and is composed of myriads of invisible electrons whirling about at a prodigious speed.

Radical changes in our thinking, and particularly in our theological thinking, are needed to catch up with this radically changed information about the Universe, for our present orthodox religious psychology is inadequate to it. If this is indeed a 'living Universe', then the concept of mind as an ever-growing force, seeking fresh horizons and enlarging its awareness, would seem more appropriate than the theological or pseudo-educational concept of mind as a sort of receptacle or wax tablet whose business it is obediently to receive instruction in fixed propositions.

In place of 'Do you believe?' a more apt criterion of salvation in future will be: 'Are you trying to learn and to deepen your understanding? Are you responding with a positive attitude to the challenge of life? Are you faithfully and continuously going forward towards such glimmerings of Light as you are capable of seeing? Are you living so that here and now, in this particular phase of being, you can begin to comprehend the meaning of eternal life?'

CHAPTER II

FROM THE LITERAL TO THE FIGURATIVE

Some things are truer than the literal truth.
GRUENBERG.

ONE VERY OBVIOUS WAY of avoiding breakdown of belief in Church doctrine would be to avoid teaching it, and this would be the recommendation of the rationalist. There is, however, a more constructive and interesting solution, the re-discovery of which we owe largely to modern psychological study of the myth. This new approach is not really new; it has been understood from time immemorial by the more perceptive religious thinkers. But it will be new to many and will offer a helpful solution to those who seek an alternative to a negative agnosticism.

Christianity is often referred to as a 'revealed religion', but what is revealed must vary with the individual's capacity to receive revelation; with his level of development, power of insight, and profundity of thought. An ancient tradition tells us that 'one esoteric truth is more precious than innumerable exoteric doctrines'. The Christian story should represent something less exoteric, something more inwardly meaningful to the mature man than it does to the child, provided that he has taken the same trouble over his inner growth as he normally does over his outer achievement. Let us look at a simple illustration of this process.

To a very young child, a picture is seen as so many disconnected objects: a man, a horse, a road. Later he is able to describe these objects: 'The man is riding the horse along the road.' Later still, if his development continues, he tries to interpret, to ascribe a meaning to the picture: 'The man is riding the horse along the road quickly because he wants to get home to his wife.'

This same enlargement of apprehension should take place in the sphere of religion, and lead to a gradual unfolding of the hidden mysteries in the Christian story; otherwise we get grown men and women still holding to childish religious concepts. The Church obstructs growth process when it places the main emphasis on certain dubiously historical facts, and offers salvation through an unreflecting effort and adventurous search. But Christianity is not at its deeper levels a matter of belief in dogma; it is a matter of insight into the inner meanings of life, and of finding through personal experience the correspondences between those meanings and the doctrinal expression of them, where such correspondences exist; of finding the truths that lie deeper than the literal truth. We encourage scientific exploration into the nature of the external world, into atomic energy and nuclear fission, regardless of whether we have the spiritual discernment to make wise use of our findings. But enquiry into the nature and energy of the soul is still frowned upon as dangerous.

This insistence on unquestioning belief in the literal, with its corresponding failure to encourage personal research, results in early defection from the Church by the critically minded. The case of Henry is a fair illustration.

He was the son of agnostic parents, and at the age of eleven, driven by that natural curiosity which urges intelligent children to find out all they can about their world, he expressed a desire to go to church. On his return home, he said to his mother: 'Do they really think that their Lord is looking down the steeple listening to all that gibberish?' Later on in the day he remarked: 'I've got into a thinking mood, and I've been thinking out what I shall write down about Heaven and Hell. Well, all those people on earth might be pointing their fingers up into the sky and saying,

43

"There is Heaven." That would be like a curled-up hedge-hog, and its spikes like fingers pointing in every direction. In that case, where is Heaven? Or you might think of two people at opposite ends of the earth, each pointing up to heaven—of course, in quite opposite directions. Then they might point downwards to Hell, and they are really pointing right through the earth into each other's Heavens. I think that jolly well puts the hat on the Devil and his family. Then again, if Heaven is up in space, it must be moving at the rate of 2,000 miles a minute. Well, no creature can live without breathing; not even fishes can. So I think their Heavens and their Hells are a pretty lot of nonsense.'

Thus did the budding rationalist polish off religion and the Church with his unanswerable logic and his literal interpretations of what he had heard. Nobody, either within the Church or without, either believer or unbeliever, explained to him that the essential truths of Christianity are independent of medieval cosmology, that he had mistaken the shadow for the substance, the mythos for the meaning, the outward and visible for the inward and spiritual. Nobody told him that, according to our degree of insight, there are endless levels of significance to be read into these non-rational, yet not unreasonable, phrases and symbols; and that the important thing is not whether we believe them literally, but whether we comprehend anything of their inner meaning.

Let it be quite clear that we are not here concerned with the factual truth of the Christian story or of official Christian dogma (which varies somewhat among Christians themselves). Such matters as the historicity and divinity of Jesus are for the historians and the theologians to contend with. Here we shall take the mythos as it stands and our only interest is with its spiritual significance. Spiritual truths are of a different order as from historical events and are not dependent on them. If Christianity does not accurately represent the drama of the soul of man, then as an inward religion it is nothing.

The symbolic approach to truth is not new. It has been

claimed that in early times Christian tradition was presented as symbolic rather than as historic truth. If that is so, we can only say that since those early times Christian thought has failed to make a clear distinction between the symbolism and the overt facts of the story, and has exalted the latter at the expense of the former. To-day there is a trend back to the earlier approach. This is illustrated in the thought of men like Dr. Albert Schweitzer: 'The abiding and eternal in Jesus is absolutely independent of historical knowledge and can only be understood by contact with His spirit which is still at work in the world. . . . It is not Jesus as historically known but Jesus as spiritually risen within men who is significant for our time and can help it. . . . A mighty spiritual force streams forth from Him. . . . This fact can neither be shaken or confirmed by any historical discovery. It is the solid foundation of Christianity.'[1]

Such questions as the nature of His relation to God and of whether it was a unique relation or one similar to that of other Avatars, are not of primary importance. To argue that He was absolutely right where all others have been only relatively right seems a little puerile and rather like an adolescent insistence that 'My man is the best'. The all-important question is not how much better He was than others, but what is the deep significance of His life and teaching for the soul of man. It is improbable that the teaching would have endured through the ages unless it expressed some basic truth about life, and certainly the power of His personality would not have affected men in the way it has unless He had lived a life in accordance with that truth.

For those to whom the symbolic approach to truth is novel, the psychology for the myth and the fairy tale will bring illumination. For example, when a child asks at the end of a fairy story, 'Is it true?' we can only answer, 'Yes and no.' Was Cinderella a real person? No; and yet it is true that the world is full of Cinderellas, of sad, inferior-feeling people who like to day-dream about reversing their role in life and becoming great and beautiful and sought-after

45

instead of neglected, used and despised. There is indeed a Cinderella in all of us. Who has not experienced 'the compensatory phantasy' at some time in their lives? Or again, let us look at the numerous stories with the theme of *The Beauty and the Beast.* Always the Prince, on whom some evil spell has been cast, cannot reveal his true nature, his good self, until the Beauty of Love has accepted him *as he is,* ugly and repulsive. Once accepted, the evil is dismissed; it vanishes into nothingness, and the Prince (the good spirit) is able to come into his own at the kiss of selfless love. But the story has a still deeper meaning. To transcend our distaste for what is beast-like in *others,* to see and love the potential beauty behind the ugliness in them, that is indeed a redemptive act. But what of the 'Beast' in ourselves? What if it needs the same recognition, acceptance, and charity? Apparently it does not get it. What we tend to do is to hide all that is beastly in ourselves both from the world and from ourselves, and concentrate busily on the evil in other people. Apparently to admit the 'ravening wolf', the shadow self, in our own natures and to be kind and yet firm with it, can be even harder than kissing the beast in another.

Periodically a literalist arises with the cry: 'Away with fairy stories! Give children only what is true, such as stories of invention and discovery.' Madame Montessori, like Mr. Gradgrind in Dickens' *Hard Times,* would give children nothing but 'facts'. The same narrow viewpoint would abolish Punch and Judy from the London parks and the 'hobgoblins and foul fiends' from Bunyan's hymn. But the literal-minded nurse who told the child to go to sleep, for 'dragons and ogres all are dead', was rebutted by the wiser father:

'Oh child, Nurse lies to thee
For dragons thou shalt see.
Please God that on that day
Thou shalt a dragon slay;
And if thou dost not faint,
God shall not want a saint.'[2]

46

And so, to Madame Montessori's assertion that fairy stories cause neuroses by preventing the child from adjusting to reality, I should reply that they do exactly the opposite: that they help us to deal with reality. For what is real? Not 'dragons and ogres' and 'ghoulies and ghosties' admittedly, but the emotional states which these monsters symbolise. To the small child, as to the adult, the emotions are overwhelmingly real, and can be terrifying. Therefore it is an immense relief to get them externalised in phantasy form. The story brings reassurance to the child in two ways. First it tells him that he is not the only one who suffers dark fears of the unknown (personified as hobgoblins, giants, witches, etc.), but that this is a universal state of affairs. Secondly, it diminishes anxiety by teaching that virtue triumphs, that there are good fairies working on the side of right and helping us to overcome our fears and wrong impulses. Children want to be good, but many of them need representatives of the super-ego in the outer world to strengthen the rather frail super-ego within, just as adults need 'angels and archangels and all the company of Heaven' to help them do battle against the powers of darkness: need to know that God exists as well as Lucifer.

The fairy story can provide for the child that confirmation, guidance and reinforcement of his own good impulses which the modern adult often mistakenly fails to give. Faith is strengthened that conflict can be satisfactorily dealt with in real life as well as in phantasy. How many children, for example, have been helped to put forth that extra ounce of effort needed for achievement by the story of the little engine puffing up the hill, cheerfully repeating to itself: 'I think I can. I think I can.'

What has all this to do with religion? Is Christianity, then, to be regarded as a fairy story, valuable only because it helps us to manage our emotional conflicts? No; it is not being suggested that Christianity is a fairy story, but that it is like one in this respect; that its deepest meaning lies hidden and must be unveiled by spiritual insight, just as the hidden

47

meaning of myth and fairy tale have, in recent years, been unveiled and brought into consciousness by psychological insight.

The language of religion is necessarily and unavoidably metaphorical for the simple reason that the highest cannot be uttered:

'To those who know Thee not, no words can paint,
And those who know Thee know all words are faint.'

It is no more possible to express all that one apprehends in religion than it is in the world of art. That is why Plato, when he came up against some mystery which he could not adequately describe, fell back on myth or allegory, for that came nearer to what he wanted to say than could any literal use of words. For the same reason, Christ gave most of His teaching in allegorical form: 'Without a parable spake He not unto them', knowing with true psychological insight that the ordinary individual will remember the images and emotions aroused by an anecdote, when he will forget or be unmoved by bald statements of fact. The parables of the Sower, the Pearl of Great Price, the Mustard Seed, the Treasure hid in the Field, the Tares and the Wheat, the Leaven in the Meal, the Marriage of the King's Son, the Labourers, the Fig Tree, the Wise and Foolish Virgins, the Lost Sheep, the Prodigal Son, the Talents, the Vineyard, the Unjust Steward, and the Last Judgement will be remembered, and with increase of understanding, long after the Creeds and the Thirty-nine Articles have been forgotten.

But not only did Jesus habitually speak in parables: His entire life-story from birth to death can be envisaged as a parable. According to the definition of the word given in childhood, 'a parable is an earthly story with a heavenly meaning'. Let us now look at some of the inner or 'heavenly' meanings in the Christian mythos itself beginning with Christmas.

Of the actual date of the birth of Jesus we know nothing.

48

The date we celebrate may have been taken over from earlier cults, since there seems no doubt that the Gospel story is to some extent eclectic. Gilbert Murray tells us that 'Many of our Christian practices come from Mithraism. The 25th of December was the birthday of Mithras; the first day of the week, dedicated to the Sun, was his holy day, as opposed to the Jewish Sabbath.'[3] Ancient Egypt also depicted the sun at the winter solstice in the form of a little child, to symbolise the coming into the world of new life and light. (It is interesting to note that very often in dream life, the image of a child carries this same symbolic significance of spiritual rebirth.)

Whatever the actual facts about the birth of the Christ Child, the story is inwardly true for this reason: the solstice in December is at the turning-point of the year, when the sun appears to move northward. The soul of man must also turn in the hardest direction (northward) in order to enter into new life; so December is symbolically accurate for the birth of the Christus, the coming of new light and life to ourselves; just as the sun causes new life to stir in the world of nature. Moreover, just as day-spring is inseparable from night and darkness, so the day-spring in the soul of man, the turning to the Light, is somehow dependent on the darkness of suffering that preceded the conversion. As Jung puts it: 'Light has need of darkness, otherwise how could it appear as Light.'[4]

This is the inner meaning of Christmas as the great mystics have understood it, and if we miss it, we miss the entire significance of the story, for, as Eckhart pertinently enquired, 'If it takes not place in me, what avails it?'

The real meaning of the doctrine of the incarnation does not lie in an outer historical event, but in an inner experience in the soul of Everyman who is ready for it. In Everyman, according to his capacity, the Word must be incarnate.

'Should Christ a thousand times be born anew,
Despair, O man, unless he's born in you,'

49

said Angelus Silesius. And another mystic, Jacob Boehme, stresses the same truth: 'The Son of God, the Eternal Word in the Father, who is the glance or brightness, and the power of the light eternal, must become man and be born in you if you will know God: otherwise you are in the dark stable and go about groping'—a vivid description of the life of many, both within and outside the mental hospitals.

No analogy is exact at every point, and the birth of the soul is not completed, like the birth of the child, in a single event. It is a continuous process, and getting 'saved' is a life-long task. 'God must be brought to birth in the soul again and again.'[5] Certainly there is the crucial moment when the choice is made between the way of life and the way of death, when the Prodigal in us decides for or against the resolution, 'I will arise'. 'A journey of a thousand miles begins with the first step', but this journey, the odyssey of the soul, is co-terminal with life: and few indeed are those who, having taken the first step, can say with Ruskin: 'I have often slipped, but have never turned my face.' The journey is also arduous, and the temptation to return to the effortless bliss of '*Eden*' is always there. But so is the angel with the flaming sword, insisting that we leave that unspoilt, unconscious, undifferentiated 'perfect' state of infancy and of tribal consciousness, and go forward into the confusion of self-conscious awareness and into the struggle and torment of the divided life; that we become striving and imperfect, but increasingly conscious individuals, in order that we may ultimately achieve the harmony and integration of the life that is united with God the Holy Spirit.

The journey is spiral rather than linear. It is definitely not circular. When Jesus urged the necessity of becoming as little children, He was obviously not advocating the road back to 'second childhood' or to the undisturbed condition of tribal semi-consciousness. That would not match the stern teaching of 'He that would save his life must lose it'. We cannot in fact become little children in the Christian sense until we have abandoned childhood and launched out

50

on the voyage of individuation which will finally bring us, in the humility, wonder, and joy of a child, to the conscious at-one-ment of the unitive life.

This birth of the soul is called a 'virgin' birth. The doctrine of the virgin birth has been a great stumbling block to many, but it ceases to be so as soon as one recognises that it refers to an inward experience and not to the birth of the body. According to the record, the Jesus of history had a human father: 'And Jacob begat Joseph, the husband of Mary, of whom was born Jesus who is called Christ.' The esoteric meaning of the Christ myth on the one hand and the factual details about the historic Jesus on the other should be clearly distinguished as belonging to different orders of being. 'Joseph', was the father of Jesus, the 'Son of man', but the title 'Son of God' refers to the 'Christus' which was born not of flesh, but of spirit.

The Christ-spirit, the Holy Spirit, the Atman, the Self (as distinct from the self), the Inner Light, or whatever other name is chosen to designate God immanent, dwells potentially and in degree in every man—a truth implicit in Jesus' promise: 'The works that I do shall ye do also.' In Him, however, as in other Avatars, the sense of union was complete, which was why He could say, 'I and My Father are one,' and could admit to Caiaphas that He was the Christ. The High Priest who thought in terms of the external did not begin to understand what He meant.

The doctrine of the virgin birth therefore refers to the spiritual, not to the material body. It does not mean that Jesus differed from other men in respect of a superhuman mode of coming into the world. Physiological facts are irrelevant to a spiritual religion, and when this Church doctrine is taken literally it carries the unfortunate suggestion that sex is impure. Its essential meaning is that, as we become illumined, earth-bound desire loses its hold, and gives place to the hunger for God and rebirth in the realm of spirit, as was explained to the uncomprehending Nicodemus. The symbolic significance of the doctrine of the virgin birth is not peculiar to Christianity. In classic mythology, the 'virgin birth' of the gods, heroes, and redeemers represents aspects or forms of new and higher potentialities in the human soul. 'It cannot be pure accident that so many ancient traditions have similar themes, that so many of them present a variety of expressions of this doctrine. The goddess Athene is reported to have been born from the head of Zeus. This version has its parallel in Hindu tradition in the birth of beings from the mind of Brahma. These are called the mind-born sons of the Creator. And Mary, the "Mother of God", the Holy Virgin, like Isis, Venus, Urania, Athene, and the virgin Diana, represents the Moon Goddess—that is, the power of consciousness in its aspect of the Tradition, ever virgin and ever young, and ever giving birth to the power of faith and insight into the mystery of life.'[6]

As a rule, when children are taught the ancient myths of gods and heroes, there is an unspoken implication that these are the funny things people used to believe about life before Christianity came into the world with 'the truth'. They should rather be taught to trace out the common thread running through all great traditions, Norse, Celtic, Classic, and especially those of the East; to find the similar meanings and values hidden behind the varied forms of expression, whenever and wherever such similarities occur. This would strengthen their interest in religion in general and illumine their understanding of Christianity in particular.

After the 'virgin' birth comes the story of the Three Wise Men, bringing their gifts, like the good fairies in myth and legend, to the newly-born Child. This is a vivid story which should be told to children just as it stands until they are ready to perceive some of its inner meanings.

Wherein lay the wisdom of these Three? First in that, although themselves men of wealth and kingly power, they recognised a greater power which dwells potentially in every helpless babe. In this particular Babe of the manger, however, their learning and wisdom were such that they had been enabled to recognise an authentic Avatar, one

52

in whom the Spirit of God was already manifest at birth.

The gifts they brought and laid in veneration before Him, all had symbolic significance. First, gold, which symbolises the sun, the source of all life. And as on the physical plane there would be no life without this golden light, so on the spiritual plane there would be no inner life without the Light of the world, the Ground or Source of all being of whom the Christus is the emblem.

A second meaning of the offering of gold might be the willingness to give up earthly possessions in exchange for the treasure of spiritual realities.

The frankincense, still used in Catholic churches, denotes the aspiration of the soul, the undying fire in the hearts of men which makes them continually strive for the truth and reach up to God through all suffering.

The myrrh, the astringent 'bitter herb', symbolises that which cleanses. It reminds us that only the pure in heart can see God, and also that pain and struggle are inseparable from creative achievement. Offering myrrh to the child meant not only that life's cup must be accepted and drained, however bitter, but that in and through such acceptance the Spirit wins power in our lives, thus making possible the life more abundant.

The mythos continues with the Temple incident at the age of twelve signifying the inevitability of the break from outer parental or scholastic, to inner authority in all healthy adolescent growth. The individual must now find out for Himself and be Himself, not a reprint of parental authority. The mother who clings and tries to hold back to protect unduly and keep things as they are, damages her Child's development.

After the Baptism of the Spirit, symbolised as the descent of a dove, came the Temptation of all young manhood to deny the Spirit, to accept worldly standards, to justify the means by the end, and suppress the highest that He knew; temptations that continually assail us all so long as we remain 'amphibious' creatures, living in what appear as divided worlds of matter and spirit.

The 'little deaths' of the Temptation—that is to say, the surrender of all that could hinder the life of the spirit—led finally to the complete surrender of the Cross and its fulfilment in the Resurrection. Our own emotional immaturity has caused us to see in the death of Christ an atonement for our sins rather than an at-one-ment with the Spirit. The guilty and legalistic concept of making payment for sin is psychologically kin to the views held by Druids, Aztecs and all primitive peoples who sacrificed human or animal lives in order to placate the gods they feared.[7] It is not a doctrine acceptable to a mature mind which would reject the idea that an innocent man should take over the consequences of his sins. No honourable individual wants another to settle his accounts for him. Neither does a loving and merciful God require that sins should be expiated in such a manner.

It may be that not many people still hold the doctrine in its crude form, but official church teaching might well do more to discourage it. The Holy Communion Service still speaks of Christ having 'made there by His one oblation of Himself once offered, a full, perfect, and sufficient sacrifice, oblation and satisfaction, for the sins of the whole world', and the Litany still pleads: 'By Thine agony and bloody sweat; by Thy cross and passion . . . Good Lord deliver us.' If these words are no longer intended to be taken at their face value, then a new interpretation of them should be made plain. The same applies to the average hymnbook, which still invites us to sing:

'He died that we might be forgiven,
    He died to make us good,
That we might go at last to Heaven,
    Saved by His precious blood.

'There was no other good enough
    To pay the price of sin;
He only could unlock the gates
    Of Heaven and let us in.'

A modern novel suggests that the only reason for singing this hymn is that it induces a certain mood of rather pleasant melancholy: 'While the hymn was being sung, Gregory whispered to Mabel: "Does your religion accept that Christ died to save the sins of the world?" Mabel shook her head and replied: "No. . . . We only sing it because it has a sad and haunting tune. We don't bother with the meaning of the words." Gregory smiled his comprehension.'[8] Such an attitude reduces the story of the Crucifixion to triviality, and this is inevitable if it has no meaning other than that implied in the usual hymns and prayers, for the modern world does not accept their teaching and therefore does not take them seriously. Christ did not die 'that we might be forgiven', for He claimed the power to forgive sins while He was still alive. Moreover, if we are to forgive 'unto seventy times seven', how much more will our Heavenly Father do the same without requiring the intermediary of a divine victim 'to be the propitiation of our sins'. Neither did He die to 'make us good' or to save us from suffering, for obviously we are not good, and we go on suffering. Why, then, did He die? Is a truer interpretation of the Passion open to us? Does Christ's death and suffering still have any significance for our age?

No one can give complete answers to these questions. We can but feel our way according to our insight and our capacity to enter into the mind of Christ and understand why He, like Socrates and Bruno, chose to suffer death rather than escape (as they might have done) or compromise with the truth they had found.

On the strength of Christ's own reported words, we can make the tentative suggestion that He believed the best way to meet a certain kind of evil was to let it have its way with you rather than try to resist it. Such directives as 'Put up thy sword' and 'Fear not them that kill the body, and after that have no more that they can do' indicate that He believed it was no use trying to meet evil by half measures; that the use of force on the earthly plane would not solve

55

the problem. One must rather go with the evil, let it have its way and 'pay the price of sin', not in order to placate an angry god, but because the power of evil, being as hideously real and terrible as it is, can only be successfully met by a greater power of good, i.e. of compassion, understanding and self-sacrifice. It was as if Christ said, 'This is the worst that evil can do, and there is no need to fear; good is stronger.' He must have believed that when love is strong enough it can contain malice and cruelty, can go right through the pain and death that these impose, and come out on the other side. In this sense it may be said that Christ 'saved' us, by going the whole way in enduring the consequences of sin and by demonstrating that evil can only be vanquished by good, *and only if we are good enough.* This was to break through something even more stupendous than the 'sound barrier', but through to what? According to the story, to a larger life, a fuller reality, a different dimension of being, pictorially referred to as Paradise.

If the story is true, therefore, we are 'saved' by the demonstration that pain and evil do not have the last word; that there is, beyond the iron gates, Something that is stronger, Something over which death itself has no dominion. To that Something, Christ confidently committed Himself. And even though for one agonising moment he lost contact with It, his final words, 'Into Thy hands,' express a calm conviction that He was going on, that He knew this life to be but a transitional stage leading to a larger life of which He had already had inner experience. It is this astounding claim, this unshaken confidence that death is not an end, that gives to the Crucifixion its special significance.

The accounts of the Resurrection and Ascension corroborate the claim and complete the story on its external side, but they are not sufficiently well authenticated to satisfy the doubter. For those who want *external* evidence of continued existence, the findings of the Society for Psychical Research in the sphere of para-psychology would

56

probably carry more weight. Subjectively speaking, the proof of immortality was given in the last words from the Cross.

The Crucifixion, then, does not represent sacrifice or vicarious suffering in the Old Testament sense of these terms —the sense that claims an atonement was once and for all made for our sins by the divine victim. If it were really true that Christ's blood could alone save and redeem mankind, it would be hard to explain the good and great men who lived before Him. Socrates claimed no certain knowledge of life after death, though what he called his Daimon, or 'sign of God within', told him that no evil could happen to a good man, that wickedness is harder to escape from than death, and that therefore at all times our first and chiefest care should be 'the perfection of our souls'. God was certainly working in the hearts of men before Christ, but unless we co-operate with the Inner Light, no god from the skies can save us in any age.

Viewing the horrors and cruelties of our time, the neo-orthodox school of Karl Barth has concluded that man is so desperately wicked, so deeply evil, that he cannot help himself, cannot pull himself up by his own bootstraps, and that is why God provided a lever, so to speak, in the person of His Son to give the necessary support to man's inadequate will. Unfortunately, as Christ Himself pointed out in the parable of the Wicked Husbandmen (Matt. xxv. 33-9), blind and evil men will pay no more attention to the king's son that to anyone else. That the brutal and arrogant feel no respect for the Jesus of history is illustrated by Hitler's jibe: 'Christ died whining on the Cross. Planetta died shouting, "Heil Hitler!"' The example of Jesus and the power of His sacrifice often work least where they are needed most. Hatred and cruelty and power-lust are not mere negative conditions; they are positive and terrible realities, and they will always lead to fresh 'crucifixions' in some form until the day dawns when good triumphs over evil everywhere as it did on the Cross of Calvary.

The true meaning of the word 'sacrifice' is to make holy or whole, or healthy, and by relating this life that we now know to the 'beyond' we dimly guess at, Christ gave us the key to this wholeness. By overcoming death, He 'opened unto us the gate of everlasting life' and showed that there is no *absolute* separation between the here and now and the life to come; that, when the obstructions are cleared away, there is, to a consciousness deepened and widened enough to perceive the fact, 'only one universe'.⁹

In the Hindu religion the story of Shiva drinking the world poison has been given the same significance as Christ drinking the Cup of Passion. The drinking is regarded as an act of sacrificial identification, not intended to 'save' us in any narrow sense, but to help us save ourselves from the dangerous and primitive aspects of our natures. The same idea is inherent in the Promethean myth; and all *mahatmas*, from Boethius to Gandhi, who have risked their lives for true values which they knew mattered more than the life of the body, have, in their degree, contributed to our redemption, *if we will be redeemed*. They have shown, as Christ did, not only that love is stronger than death, but that what is done is done for all; that one completely dedicated individual can act as a channel of grace for others, can give of his spiritual wealth on behalf of all, and so strengthen man in the way of righteousness.

> 'Through such souls as these
> God, stooping, shows sufficient of his light
> For us in the dark to rise by.'

Whatever the true and full meaning of the Crucifixion on its literal side, figuratively speaking its meaning is the same as that of the parable of the Grain of Wheat, which must fall to the ground and die before it can bring forth fruit. The new life must break through the husk of the old; one part of us must die if a new part is to live. That is the way of life, as all the mystic poets have known.

'Even as this corn,
Earth-born,
We are snatched from the sod;
Reaped, ground to grist,
Crushed and tormented in the Mills of God,
And offered at Life's hands, a living Eucharist.'[10]

The root of the matter lies not in the literal but in the spiritual truth of the Christian story; not in a dogma to be believed, but in our power of perception into the inner meanings of life and of finding, through personal experience, the correspondences between those meanings and the doctrinal expression of them, where such correspondences exist. If, for example, we have never been conscious of the temptation to take the line of least resistance, to sacrifice integrity to expediency, to use power unworthily, or to throw up the sponge and abandon our own best standards, then we shall certainly not understand the nature and meaning of Christ's wrestling with the Devil (the Shadow self) in the Wilderness. If we have never tried to transmute a negative and destructive attitude into a positive and creative one, then we shall get no further than Nicodemus in understanding the meaning of spiritual rebirth. If we have never even glimpsed another dimension of being, or been translated into ecstasy in the presence of great beauty, then the account of the Transfiguration will be just an unrealistic story of no particular significance; and if our small 'crucifixions' are regarded only as sufferings to be escaped from, and not as opportunities for creative insight, into a larger life, then Christ's death is wasted on us. Suffering is not good in itself: Christ always did what He could to minimise it. But when it cannot be cured, the only alternative is to accept it and use it as creatively as possible; going through the Vale of Misery to use it as a well. In short, to be a follower of Christ does not mean clinging to Him as a Saviour either from the wrath of God or from the evil in ourselves. It means discovering through our own effort the moral and spiritual realities that he discovered through his own personal effort: it means trying to live our lives courageously as he did; otherwise we can but have a valueless verbal knowledge of those realities. For 'Knowledge is a function of being' and we can know just as much of spiritual truth as our stage of development, our capacity for insight, our achievement of wisdom and our understanding of love have equipped us to apprehend; no more. Therefore instead of the rather trite enquiry: 'Are you a Christian?' a more intelligent though equally unanswerable question would be 'How much of a Christian are you?'

The failure to understand the metaphorical language of the mythos, the failure to realise that the messages from Reality come to us first in an outward form whose inner meaning and beauty we must gradually learn to apprehend as our inner life develops, causes not only an enormous and unnecessary amount of scepticism, tragic loss of faith, and hostility to institutional religion; it also causes unnecessary division between good men with the same basic philosophy of life. The humanist Gilbert Murray, speaking of his closeness of outlook with his sincere Christian friends who make a stand for values in the face of public opinion, writes: 'This is the army to which I belong, the faith for which I stand. In such cases we, the humanists and the real Christians, find ourselves together. There is agreement, as the psychologists say, below the threshold, an agreement belonging to the same region as the emotions roused by great works of art. . . . Where then does the difference come? Simply in the reasons which we give for believing that this faith is right. . . . It is the myth that divides us.'[11]

It is the claim of this book that the myth need not and should not divide; that it only does so because the mind of man has a great need of the concrete and the personal, and that in order to satisfy this need, he unconsciously turns what was originally intended as a figurative expression of the otherwise inexpressible into a statement of objective fact. It is an easy thing to do, but it is self-defeating, for the conscious part of the mind is also capable of reason, and will ultimately be obliged to question these 'objective facts'.

In the course of its history, the Church has been guilty of this reactionary tendency, of turning living truth into a Procrustean bed of dead dogma. It has insisted that we believed in such impossibilities as 'the Father incomprehensible, the Son incomprehensible, and the Holy Ghost incomprehensible'. Worse still, in the name of truth and righteousness, it has liquidated and threatened with eternal punishment of considerable severity those who showed signs of independent thought. Not merely to perish, but to 'perish everlastingly' may sound like a contradiction in terms, since to perish is to end, but it was the best revenge the zealot could think of for those who had the effrontery to differ from him.

For the zealot's apparent concern with truth is but a cover for his real concern, the enhancement and protection of his own ego. So when he lost the battle for domination in the sphere of religion (where, if the threat of Athanasius is still heard, modern man finds it amusing rather than alarming, and less likely of fulfilment than the execution orders of the Duchess in *Alice*), that was not a clear gain in the growth of toleration. He merely shifted his sphere of operations over to politics where nonconformity is now punishable with equal ferocity (though in this life only) in the cause of humanitarianism. Presumably the fanatic really sees himself as a lover of men when he consigns some of them to Siberia or to the concentration camp 'for the welfare of the whole'. The mind of the fanatic might be rendered a little more flexible if he was trained in childhood to distinguish in every sphere between statements which are permissibly dogmatic and those which must be hypothetical, tentative or metaphorical. Science can with justice make literal and dogmatic assertions about that which is verifiable by scientific test and measurement. If a specimen of argon is shown to have a certain atomic weight, no one will question the fact. But to make dogmatic statements about the best

61

style and method of organisation for society, or about the great mystery of life, is a form of fundamentalism as stupid and intolerant as that of the 'Bible Christian' who degrades a great literature into something which must be uncritically believed 'from cover to cover'. All great allegories illumine; they do not try to tell in exact terms. Dante's *Divine Comedia*, Bunyan's *Pilgrim's Progress*, Homer's *Odyssey*, Browning's *Paracelsus*, Blake's poetry, and so on, all give us pictures rather than maps of life. We realise it does not matter whether Odysseus resisted a real Circe, Syrens or Polyphemus. The point of the allegory is, like that of Jacob wrestling with the dark angel, that it is true to the trials and temptations of life as we know them. The same applies to Christianity. If when we ask, 'Is it true?' we mean, 'Is it historically established?', we make the outward and visible of greater importance than the inward and spiritual. This is a materialist rather than a sacramentalist approach. But if we mean, 'Is the teaching true? Is the order of nature really a moral order? Is right action really treasured in the nature of things? Does the whole saga of the birth, life and death of Jesus constitute a true allegory of the inner life-journey of every human being?' then we are asking spiritually significant questions—questions to which we must each find the answer for ourselves.

The rationalist may reasonably ask at this point: 'If the mythos leads to so much confusion by being interpreted literally, why not discard it? If what the religionist is really concerned with is spiritual meanings and values, why confuse the issue with reference to dubiously historical events, to symbols and rituals? Why not say as exactly as possible what you mean without dressing it all up in story and imagery? Let us have a purely ethical Church and be done with futile argument.'

One answer to these sensible questions has already been given—namely, that there are meanings and experiences in life which cannot be expressed in accurate, factual statements, but can be at least partially expressed in poetic or

62

story form. The myth, therefore, is no less valuable for not being 'scientific'.

The second justification of the use of pictorial metaphor lies in the limitations of the human mind. If we were pure spirits and could receive spiritual truth direct, then presumably we could do without these symbols and allegories. The deepest form of awareness is imageless, and if we were all like the few who are capable of imageless thought, then we could get along happily with abstract terms. But most of us need the support of imagery to carry our meanings and our intuitive intimations of the unseen. Indeed, it might be argued that a reality which is timeless and spaceless can only be referred to in symbolic form by creatures limited to time and space. In one of the Apocryphal Gospels there is a story of how the child Jesus, picking up the clay sparrows with which the other boys were playing, threw them into the air, where they became living birds. We can read this as an absurdity or as an example of Christ's magical powers, or as a parable of profound meaning.

We noted earlier in the chapter how Jesus used the allegorical method continuously in His teaching, and to-day analytic psychology, especially that of Carl Jung, has brought us fresh illumination as to the power of the image, and fresh insight into the lost meaning of the old mythologies and their relationship to the subways of our hidden selves. At bottom we all have the same kind of problems: all, for instance, must grope their way through the dark maze of circumstance until they come out into the Light, and therefore the myth of Ariadne, feeling her way out of the Cretan labyrinth by keeping contact with the guiding thread, speaks to the condition of all. So does Blake's imagery on the same theme:

'I will give you a golden string,
Only wind it into a ball:
It will bring you in at Jerusalem
Right under Heaven's wall.'

And the myth of Persephone tells us that our dark times are not wasted, that something is going on underground; that even though we can see no light and observe no progress, yet 'we live in the night-time also' because the seed begins its growth underground. It is not surprising that most agricultural communities have worshipped a god of spring, who saves the world from the barren and fruitless winter. The story of Christ's death and Resurrection carries this myth on to another plane. 'The day-spring from on high hath visited us, to be a light to them that sit in darkness and in the shadow of death.' Another thing that the myth demonstrates, often in our dreams, is that we all have within us the emotional states which these personifications express, not only a lost Ariadne, a nostalgic Eurydyce, an ambitious Icarus, but a Castor and a Pollux, a Loki and a Baldur, an Adam and a Christus *in potentia*: that the myth of Lucifer is re-enacted in modern dress, not only in the lives of notorious dictators, but in the lives of all of us when we want to assert power over others and to impose our 'truth' on them.

We have become sadly cut off from these images with their wealth of meaning, and from our own unconscious minds where they arise. Therefore we have now to establish the connection consciously in order to revitalise the dead images and make them the chalice of the spirit of life. Modern study of the dream is helping to do this. It shows the dream to be a form of myth whose inner meaning lies hidden in the manifest content and in the imagery employed. If we are cut off from that meaning, the power it could yield is lost to us; but if we dwell with our dream images, they may gradually reveal their significance to us, as they did to Joseph.

Professor Dixon writes: 'The most powerful force in the making of history has been . . . metaphor, figurative expression. It is by imagination that men have lived: imagination rules all our lives. The human mind is not, as philosophers would have you believe, a debating hall, but a picture gallery.'[12] In fact, it is both, but if the pictures in the gallery no longer say anything, they might as well be removed. In an old village church in England, a visitor once noticed that each member of the congregation habitually bowed to a certain place on a blank wall. When questioned, no one could offer any explanation for this ritual beyond saying that it had always been done. Some time later, redecoration involved scraping the wall, and this revealed a sacred painting, the original object of the veneration, which had continued by a kind of automatic perseveration long after its significance was lost and forgotten.

This atrophy is taking place all the time. To the average Protestant church-goer, the church building and everything in it has lost the wealth of meaning it once carried, a wealth which enriched the minds of those who understood it. Even such simple things as the Easter egg, the gargoyle, dart, eagle, pelican, dove, lion and lamb, and the cross in all its varied forms, are for many to-day dead images. This would not matter so much if we had not lost contact with that creative part of our minds which continually produces fresh imagery. But since this is so, and while we are trying to restore the connection, we can try to recover the meaning of the images we semi-consciously employ from long habit. For their meaning is eternal, and new images can but reinforce, not improve on, the life and death story of, for example, the grain of wheat and its symbolisation of the Christian drama and the drama of all human life; that we must 'fall' and die to live, 'have by losing, and hold by letting go'. This parable of the Grain of Wheat seems rather grim and alarming unless accompanied by the complementary idea that our loss may ultimately prove to be a gain, that detachment and attachment can be part of a balanced process in which we give up the lesser for the sake of the greater good. Otherwise we land in an asceticism which gives up for the sake of giving up and gambles on a better time in the world to come. A subtle form of spiritual pride soon creeps in on such purely negative self-denial.

When we keep the image and lose sight of that for which

it stands, there is danger of real idolatry, of valuing the image higher than its meaning. We sing in cheerful superiority that:

> 'The heathen in his blindness
> Bows down to wood and stone,'

but is the heathen essentially different from the Christian, when the latter allows the image to detract attention from that which it represents? St. Bernard once wrote: 'So great and marvellous a variety of diverse forms meets the eye, that one is tempted . . . to pass the whole day looking at these carvings rather than in meditating on the law of God.'

A further and more serious danger follows this tendency to idolise the image in and for itself. Dissociated from its original meaning, it may be used as a cover for personal and ignoble ends. It is a commonplace of history that the Christian Cross, essentially the symbol of sacrificial love, has been degraded into a banner for 'holy' wars fought in its name. And in one of Goya's most horrifying drawings, 'Que Crueldad', we see above the suffering Victim the Cross on behalf of which He is being tortured. Hitler hid his paranoiac lust for racial domination under the swastika, and all national flags are in danger of waving a similar message to 'My country, right or wrong', and so earning the same fate. When a flag begins to be treated with reverent awe as a thing sacred in itself, then it becomes painfully easy to slip into the assumption that whatever is done under its aegis must not be criticised, for the flag is above criticism, it can do no wrong. The same dishonesty is at times apparent in the use of certain words, such as 'freedom' or 'democracy'. These are good words; therefore whatever is done in their name must also be good. Conversely, the symbol can suffer from 'guilt by association' and come to be regarded as evil in itself. So Cromwell, like a child who will punish the chair that has hurt him, punished the beautiful churches of his

66

day. But the image-laden churches were not guilty; they had merely been abused, and the answer to misuse is right use, not abolition or defacement.

We cannot do without symbols, image and metaphor, because we cannot think of the deeper things of life without their aid. Embryonic and limited creatures as we are, we cannot and should not expect to do more than begin to apprehend reality. We must use such terms and images as seem most nearly to express its nature. Jesus taught that God is Spirit, but this statement is an exceedingly difficult one to fill with content unless we personalise Spirit. Jesus also said, 'When ye pray, say 'Our Father . . .' Ramakrishna, the great Indian saint, found it more natural to think of God as 'Mother'. The Roman Catholic Church would appear to do both.

No analogy could possibly be complete or accurate. Whatever the nature of God, the Ultimate Reality, it must be something vastly different from that of an earthly parent, and vastly different from anything we can envisage. Indeed it is not surprising that for many the image of God as a loving father is unacceptable because it does not seem consonant with the misery and suffering they see around them. These, if they conceive God at all, will prefer to use such remote and impersonal terms as the 'Absolute' or the 'Life Force'.

Certain it is that, if God exists, if there is a greater Reality corresponding to our intuitions, then there must be some sense in which He is an indwelling spirit in all of life, not 'throned above the skies' *in absentia*. In that case our aim will be to see not only the language and ritual of the Church, but the whole of life as sacramental: 'Every common bush afire with God'; 'Tongues in trees, books in running brooks, sermons in stones, and good in everything'; all creation a living universe, the abode of the indwelling Logos; 'every thing, event, or thought, a point of intersection between creature and Creator . . . a doorway through which a soul may pass out of time into eternity'.[13]

67

CHAPTER III

FROM THE INTELLECTUAL TO THE EMPIRICAL

As the true method of knowledge is experiment; the true faculty
of knowledge must be the faculty which experiences.

WILLIAM BLAKE.

THERE ARE VARIED ways of acquiring knowledge, among
which we may distinguish at least four. There is the way of
sense experience: if we want to know whether it is raining,
we look out of the window in the sure belief that 'seeing is
believing'. Actually, the senses are not always so reliable as
we assume. When the Crystal Palace was burnt down,
observers 'saw' the monkeys writhing in terror on the high
bars under the roof. Later it transpired they were not
monkeys; only bits of material.

Secondly, there is the way of authority. The child asks his
parents, the pupil his teacher, the patient his doctor, the
novice her priest, the fundamentalist his Bible, the Com-
munist his *Daily Worker*, and so on. This is an indirect and
secondary road to knowledge, essential under some circumstances, justifiable under others, but a way to be outgrown
by the individual capable of seeking the truth for himself.

Thirdly, there is the way of reason, when, in order to
reach a conclusion on some matter, we try to think it
through in accordance with the universally accepted laws of
thought. If we break any of those laws by, for example,
introducing a four-term syllogism, the conclusion is not
acceptable to reason. Nobody questions the validity of the
laws of logic to which the reasoning process must adhere;

68

the differences of opinion arise only over the major premisses and how they are arrived at. This brings us to the last avenue to knowledge, the way of intuition.

In reasoning, we use that part of our mind known as the foreconscious or the critical intellect, corresponding to that part of our brain known as the frontal cortex. This use marks an immense advance in man's evolution. The ability to think for oneself independently of the tribe is a comparatively late achievement, and one bought at the cost of much persecution and suffering. No wonder then that man values his intellect and reasoning powers, and believes them to be not only the method *par excellence*, but the only valid method for acquiring reliable information. No wonder that he rather fiercely disparages anything that looks like a backward step and questions the truth of anything which cannot be tested in the laboratory or proved by the strict processes of logical reasoning. No wonder he steers clear of terms as indefinable as intuition or as incomprehensible as mysticism, and is even a little sceptical of imagination or of the value of aesthetic as compared with intellectual experience.

And there is another basis to his scepticism. He has observed that the phrase 'My intuition tells me' is often used as an alibi for clear, hard thinking by those who want something to be as their 'intuition' tells them; and he will recall that a recent tyrant who brought the world to the brink of ruin, gloried in his intuitive 'hunches' and made the proud boast, 'I think with my guts.' Someone has caustically remarked that the main lesson taught by higher education is not to let oneself be duped, and if, under the cloak of this vague and equivocal term, 'intuition', people dupe themselves and others, why should we not be chary of it?

Yet, in fact, nobody is a pure 'intellectual', a thinking machine who relies for all information on his reason alone. The critical intelligence can only take us so far, and then reaches an impasse. Even with the greatest of thinkers there comes a stage when they are blocked and must await an inspiration, the illumination of a new idea which will throw fresh light on the problem. We do not know how this imaginative leap or intuitive apprehension functions; all we know is that it is not the conclusion of a syllogism, that it seems to come from some other and deeper part of the mind than the conscious intellect. Newton was not reasoning when he suddenly 'saw' that the planets are being pulled towards each other as the apple is being 'pulled' to the ground. He did not think it out; it came to him as a fantastic guess, though a great deal of hard thinking had preceded the insight.

This particular form of intuitional experience has been called by Radakrishnan 'Integral thought' as distinct from critical analytic thought, because it brings things together in a new pattern, integrates them rather than breaks them up into parts, as does analytic thought. It reveals the pieces as integral to a larger setting or pattern which relates them all into a meaningful whole. This creative insight seems to come from a deep unconscious part of the mind with which we are not in touch save at the moment of illumination. Several great thinkers such as Poincaré and Hamilton have described this process taking place in themselves when they could go no further with their own conscious reasoning.

In the sphere of religion the corresponding experience is given the name 'mysticism'. This can be conscious or unconscious. Apprehensions of the unseen; a sense of harmonious unity with a larger life—these are experienced with varying degrees of vividness by the tribal consciousness before it is broken up in the painful but necessary process of individuation. They are also experienced by the little child before the dawn of self-conscious awareness and questioning. Leaving this 'Golden Age' of perfect harmony with life is painful, but essential in the cause of development. In the process of outgrowing the unconscious 'perfection' of child or tribal life, in order to become an individual, the mind that was once whole and all of a piece becomes divided; the forebrain develops, and we speak of the conscious and the unconscious mind as if they were separate entities. In

70

that sense, we might all be called 'split personalities'. The search for conscious reintegration with the whole is long and arduous, and involves us in much confusion. When in the sphere of religion man breaks with the forms and traditions of the past, he may lose his anchorage so completely that he, as we say, breaks down. So does the tribe when its traditional mythology is challenged. Or he may experiment for himself, daringly and perhaps dangerously, until, with good fortune, he passes from the life that is divided into the life that is united, and becomes as full of peace and wonder and confidence in life as the little child before the latter lost his sense of wholeness. The struggle and confusion are the price we pay for this enlargement of consciousness. With greater wisdom, the price would not need to be so high nor the struggle so painful.

At times, the fear of anarchy, of unrestrained individualism, causes authority to call a halt to freedom for personal exploration. At one time of his life, Martin Luther, himself a mystic, claimed that nobody can receive anything from the Holy Ghost unless he experiences it. But when he saw individual expression running rampant as a result of his teaching, he swung back strongly to the 'safe' way of authoritarian tradition. And, indeed, it is in the main true that only those should leave the trodden path who have already achieved well disciplined ego-structures, capable of standing alone and continuing their development without the support of the group. Buddha likened the structure of religious doctrine to a raft which can be thrown away when one has crossed over to the other side of the stream. But not all can make the crossing, and in any case it is disastrous to abandon the raft in midstream without any reliable alternative support in the form of personal intuitive experience of a larger life than that of the shore he is leaving: for it is on this alone that the independent explorer can rely, guided by the torch of the great mystics who have preceded him.

It has been said that a truer keynote for our age than the intellectual approach of Descartes' 'Cogito ergo sum' ('I think, therefore I am'), is the conative and affective approach of *'Respondeo, etsi mutabor'* ('I answer, though I have to change'; I listen and I answer to those intimations of another dimension of being, even though such response means that I must enlarge and refashion my own consciousness). The story of St. Paul reversing his way of life in response to the 'heavenly vision', and striving henceforth to follow the way of love instead of the way of fascist domination, is an illustration of this process on the grand scale. For most people the task of the religious life is a matter of continuous small changes, of clearing away the undergrowth of 'tares' in the emotional life until our intuitive perceptions become as reliable as our rational processes. In this task reason and intuition, critical thought and feeling response, are complementary rather than mutually exclusive. We do not have to choose between them, but to 'marry' them to each other, if we would achieve ever wider apprehensions through integral thought. Intuition must be constantly checked and scrutinised by the critical intellect; intellect must be constantly enriched by the new life brought to it through intuition. Reason can keep the soil of the mind in good order, but it can plant no new life therein.

In addition to needing constant check from the critical intellect, intuition, to be reliable, must be nurtured by good feeling. At the present stage of our lopsided development, it would seem that intuition is more important in the sphere of human relations than in any other. For in this sphere people tend to rely rather too confidently on immediate impressions. 'I saw right away what he was like'; 'I can always tell at once whether I like a person or not'; such statements might conceivably have validity if the person making them not only had unusual powers of insight, but also a very stable and warm-hearted emotional constitution. The intuitions of an unloving and distrustful individual could not in the nature of things be reliable, for he sees through a damaged instrument. His fears will make him primarily sensitive to that which he fears, and he is likely to see, and therefore to educe, only the negative emotions in others. 'It is wisdom to believe the heart'—yes, but only if the heart is motivated by an outgoing understanding love, for without love and emotional integrity no valid intuitive response is possible in the sphere of human relations. So whatever the exact nature of intuition, 'the faculty which experiences', we can at least say this: that its validity depends on clear thinking and on good feeling. Intuition is not a complete thing in itself that one either has or does not have, like hearing and vision. Its strength and its quality in any individual are proportionate to the clarity of his thinking, the integrity of his feeling, and the strength of his loving, for 'Love is swift of foot' both in telling us what is needed and in how best to meet the need.

Love is a large matter of which we know very little, save that there is general agreement among those entitled to our deferential attention that it is more important than anything else in life. After a life of unwavering intellectual search, Bertrand Russell has recently expressed his arrival at the same conclusion: 'The root of the matter', he writes, 'is a very simple and old-fashioned thing, a thing so simple that I am almost ashamed to mention it, for fear of the derisive smile with which wise cynics will greet my words. The thing I mean—please forgive me for mentioning it—is love, Christian love or compassion. If you feel this, you have a motive for existence, a guide in action, a reason for courage, an imperative necessity or intellectual honesty.'[1] In other words, if you have this Christian love in you, you have all that matters; this is what the fourteenth-century mystic meant when he wrote, 'By love thou shalt find him, but by thought never',[2] though a more exact statement would be 'by thoughtful love or by loving thought', since truth must be sought and served with all that we are, head and heart.

The tendency of much education in the past has been to stress the intellectual, and almost completely ignore the feeling and experiencing aspects of mind. Our reliance on

73

the spoken word is unbounded, so much so that in some circles whenever national morality seems to be sinking to 'a new low' there is a clamour for stricter attendance at church or Sunday school, where children will be taught once again their moral duty by exposure to the words of the Catechism, the Ten Commandments, and/or the Sermon on the Mount—all of which is waste of time unless it is related to and interpreted in the light of their personal experience. The saying, 'There is no teaching, there is only learning', really means that the word taught should be a clarification, summary, and an illumination of experience; it cannot be used as a substitute for it. The truth about love or any other value can only be learnt through the long, slow, difficult process of practising it, just as one could only learn to play the violin by practising, not by listening to dissertations about it.

The state of the world is a sad commentary on two thousand years of Christian teaching that love is the root of the matter, the solution to all problems. Part of the explanation of our failure lies in this educational fallacy, based on a lazy hope, that words can be a short cut, a substitute for living experience. All teachers know that it is much easier to tell children what we believe is right than to 'waste time' letting them discuss a matter for themselves and perhaps arrive at no conclusion: that it is less confusing and untidy, and also perhaps more pleasing to authority, to teach by talking from a desk than to go to the trouble of arranging experiences through which children may learn for themselves of those things to which our words refer. This, of course, does not mean that children can or should rediscover all knowledge for themselves. The heuristic method has its obvious limitations and the spoken word has its very valuable place, but in the sphere of moral and religious education, if the word is divorced from life, it is sounding brass. The roots of the life of the spirit must be nourished in experience if the fruits are to be healthy, and only by building up strong, positive, loving and creative emotions in children can we

74

save them from being overwhelmed by the destructive powers that lie hidden but alive in all of us.

All great educators have known and stressed the importance of the feeling and experiencing sides of life, and have tried to redress the imbalance of the past which over-emphasised the verbal, the intellectual, and the utilitarian. But the battle is never finally won. There is a strong movement in America at the moment against 'Deweyism', especially on the part of those employers who feel the main business of education is to produce literate secretaries. They are quite right that children should learn how to read and write and spell correctly, but 'these ought ye to have done and not to have left the other [the education of the emotions] undone'; for the latter, as John Dewey well knew, is considerably the more important.

Another cause of our failure lies in the fatal tendency to split up life's experiences into isolated compartments and label them this or that, as if they existed independently of each other. But just as words cannot effectively be separated from experience, and just as religious values cannot rightly be separated from those that are intellectual, aesthetic, moral and spiritual, neither can these latter be separated from each other. Differentiate we must, ever more and more, in the service of clarity, but what is distinguishable in thought is not always separable in fact, and the interrelationship of the eternal verities has been pointed out by many a philosopher and poet. Jesus said, 'The truth shall make you free,' and, conversely, without freedom we cannot find truth. Whitehead adds that beauty is essential because 'In the absence of beauty, truth sinks to triviality',³ and therefore, 'apart from beauty, truth is neither good or bad'. Keats makes the simple claim that 'Beauty is truth, truth beauty', and Plato agrees that 'the good is the beautiful,' καλὸς κἄγαθός. To St. Paul's assertion that love is the supreme value, giving life to all others, Lao-tzu adds the experience of joy: and tells us: 'There is no greater joy than love of goodness.' So while we now look at these religious values under separate headings, let us remember that in life they are not separate but are organically related, both to each other, to all life, and to the Source of all; that goodness, beauty, love, joy, truth, are facets of the Holy Spirit, and that experience of them constitutes the only matrix in which the heart of things can be revealed. If we miss this relatedness, if we live partial lives at the periphery instead of from the Source or Centre, if we are concerned only with goodness like the Puritans, or only with knowledge like Faust, or with beauty like Cellini, our vision will suffer accordingly and we shall achieve neither intuitive insight nor spiritual maturity. For 'goodness' alone degenerates into a narrow piety; beauty alone into aestheticism; knowledge alone into academic formalism.

Therefore the clever must try to be good, and the good, *pace* Kingsley, must be as clever as they can, and both must joyously care for beauty. To care for only one value is to live always in one room and to see a single view, when out on the roof we might glimpse the Whole.

CHAPTER IV

EXPERIENCE OF LOVE: STUMBLING-BLOCKS IN LEARNING TO LOVE

The unloved cannot love.

WILLIAM BLAKE.

THE EXPERIENCE OF being loved is the most important experience in a child's life, but 'love' is perhaps the most ambiguous and overworked word in our language. It connotes every shade of friendly feeling from mild interest to deep, lifelong concern; from clinging dependence on others to a great-hearted desire to serve them; from passionate possessiveness to selfless devotion. The same word may also be used to refer to chocolate cake or to the Illyrian coastline; to fresh asparagus or to a statue by Rodin. We 'love' them all. St. Thomas Aquinas is said to have used the word 'nature' with forty different meanings; it would seem that the word 'love' is required to carry even more. The Greeks had at least two words, *eros* and *agape*, by which to distinguish between the emotional states of a Casanova and a Gandhi, a Don Juan and a Florence Nightingale. Since we have only one, we must try to differentiate its various meanings as well as we can. About the desirability, beauty and value of love at its higher levels, great minds have written and spoken throughout the ages. It would indeed be superfluous to try and add to the sublime and eternal utterances of Jesus, Paul, Shakespeare, Traherne or John of the Cross. We all thrill to their words and subscribe to their teaching. The trouble is, we seem incapable of following it. As Pascal remarked, 'All the great maxims have been spoken: it

77

remains only to put them into practice', and as the child of six said to her mother, who was explaining the teachings of Jesus to her: 'Yes; I understand. He wanted people to love each other. What a pity it didn't work.' Our problem is that of discovering where and how and why we go so wrong in the process of loving.

In this chapter we shall try to be specific, to remember the warning of Zen Buddhism, 'Beware of abstractions', and to illustrate some of the particular ways in which we unwittingly damage the capacity for love in young children, inhibit their feeling-awareness and blunt the sensitivity of their response to and delight in the outgoing love of another. For once this capacity is warped in infancy, the individual may, as Froebel's insight saw long ago, arrive at adulthood incapable of loving. In the *Mutter und Kose Lieder* he tells us—

> 'Even the child's love left unsought,
> Unfostered, droops and dies away.'

If that happens, what boots it to teach or preach on the duty of loving? The individual may long for love, but he has become emotionally paralysed.

Fortunately, this fact of early frustration is being very forcibly brought home to us to-day by careful scientific studies. In her book, *The Rights of Infants*, Dr. Margaret Ribble gives a spectacular illustration of the deprivation of love and its effects on the physical and mental health of the child:

'Little Bob was born in the maternity hospital where the writer was making studies of infants at the time. He was a full-term child and weighed six pounds three ounces at birth. During the two weeks' stay in the hospital, the baby was breast-fed and there was no apparent difficulty with his body functions. The mother, a professional woman, had been reluctant about breast feeding because she wished to take up her work as soon as possible after the baby was born, but she yielded to the kindly encouragement of the hospital nurses, and the feeding was successful. Both mother and child were thriving when they left the hospital. On returning home, the mother found that her husband had suddenly deserted her, the climax of an unhappy and maladjusted marriage relationship. She discovered soon after that her milk did not agree with the baby. As is frequently the case, the deep emotional reaction had affected her milk secretion. The infant refused the breast and began to vomit. Later he was taken to the hospital and the mother did not call to see him. At the end of a month, she wrote that she had been seriously ill and asked the hospital to keep the child until further notice.

'In spite of careful medical attention and skilled feeding, this baby remained for two months at practically the same weight. He was in a crowded ward and received very little personal attention. The busy nurses had no time to take him up and work with him as a mother would, by changing his position and making him comfortable at frequent intervals. The habit of finger-sucking developed, and gradually the child became what is known as a ruminator, his food coming up and going down with equal ease. At the age of two months he weighed five pounds. The baby at this time was transferred to a small children's hospital, with the idea that this institution might be able to give him more individual care. It became apparent that the mother had abandoned the child altogether.

'When seen by the writer, this baby actually looked like a seven months' foetus, yet he had also a strange appearance of oldness. His arms and legs were wrinkled and wasted, his head large in proportion to the rest of his body, his chest round and flaring widely at the base over an enormous liver. His breathing was shallow, he was generally inactive, and his skin was cold and flabby. He took large quantities of milk, but did not gain weight, since most of it went through him with very little assimilation and with copious discharges of mucus from his intestines. The baby showed at this time the pallor which in our study we have found typical of

79

infants who are not mothered, although careful examination of his blood did not indicate a serious degree of anaemia. He was subject to severe sweating, particularly during sleep. A thorough study showed no indication of tuberculosis. The child's abdomen was large and protruding, but this proved to be due to lax intestinal muscles and consequent distention with gas and to a greatly enlarged and distended liver, which was actually in proportion to that of the foetus. There was no evidence of organic disease, but growth and development were definitely at a standstill, and it appeared that the child was gradually slipping backward to lower and lower levels of body economy and function.

'The routine treatment for this hospital for babies who are not gaining weight is to give them concentrated nursing care. They are held in the nurses' laps for feeding and allowed at least half an hour to take the bottle. From time to time their position in the crib is changed, and when possible the nurse carries them about the ward for a few minutes before and after each feeding. This is the closest possible approach to mothering in a busy infants' ward. Medical treatment consists of frequent injections of salt solution under the skin to support the weakened circulation in the surface of the body. With this treatment, the child began to improve slowly. As his physical condition became better, it was possible for our research group to introduce the services of a volunteer "mother", who came to the hospital twice daily in order to give him some of the attention he so greatly needed. What she actually did was to hold him in her lap for a short period before his 10 a.m. and 6 p.m. feedings. She was told that he needed love more than he needed medicine, and she was instructed to stroke the child's head gently and speak or sing softly to him and walk him about. Her daily visits were gradually prolonged until she was spending an hour twice a day, giving the baby this artificial mothering. The result was good. The child remained in the hospital until it was five months of age, at which time he weighed nine pounds. All rumination and diarrhoea had stopped, and he had become an alert baby with vigorous muscular activity. His motor co-ordinations were, of course, retarded. Although he held up his head well and looked about, focusing his eyes and smiling in response to his familiar nurses, he could not yet grasp his own bottle or turn himself over, as is customary at this age. The finger-sucking continued, as is usually the case with babies who have suffered early privation.

'In accordance with the new hospital procedure, as soon as the child's life was no longer in danger, he was transferred to a good, supervised foster-home in order that he might have still more individual attention. Under this régime his development proceeded well, and gradually he mastered such functions as sitting, creeping and standing. His speech was slow in developing, however, and he did not walk until after the second year. The general health of this child is now excellent at the end of his third year; also his I.Q. is high on standard tests, but his emotional life is deeply damaged. With any change in his routine, or with a prolonged absence of the foster-mother, he goes into a state which is quite similar to a depression. He becomes inactive, eats very little, becomes constipated and extremely pale. When his foster-mother goes away, he usually reacts with a loss of body-tone and alertness, rather than with a definite protest. His emotional relationship to the foster-mother is receptive, like that of a young infant, but he makes little response to her mothering activities except to function better when she is there. He has little capacity to express affection which he so deeply needs. Without the constant friendly explanations of the situation from the visiting nurse, she would probably have given up the care of the child.'[1]

It would be going too far to assert that little Bob will never become capable of loving. One cannot foretell such things with absolute certainty. What does seem certain is that his love will always have in it a large element of dependency and clinging; and that the wasting disease called marasmus, from which he so nearly died, has its counterpart in a kind of marasmus of the soul, which like the body, becomes scarred and remains immature when deprived of its rightful nourishment of love. We have already referred to the research work of Anna Freud in this connection and to the paralysis of the emotional life which can result from a too frequent break in the love relationship. This, however, is not the worst that can happen. Apathy at least does no positive harm to anyone else; but a bitter hate, a smouldering resentment which misses no opportunity for hitting back as and where it can, may make life a misery, not only for the poor emotional cripple himself, but for everyone who comes within the range of his influence. Indeed, as we of this age know to our cost the range of that influence may be world-wide and appalling in its effects. Studies of Hitler indicate that what this paranoic was really doing when he set out to conquer the world was saying in effect to his disparaging father: 'I'll show you whether I'm any good or not.'

It behoves us, then, to look well into the causes of love's failure in the early stages of the child's life, for to undo the damage accomplished then is a gigantic and sometimes, it seems, an impossible task. St. John of the Cross, with profound insight, gave the directive: 'Where there is no love, put in love, and you will find love'—like priming a pump— but there are not many among us saintly enough to love the loveless back into lovability, or wise enough to know how to do it.

In the past people have tended to suppose that the importance of a person was proportionate to his age and size; that no mental life of any significance took place in the human organism until he was able to express his feelings in words. 'I didn't know it would have a brain,' commented a small boy when his baby sister surprised him with a responsive smile. That has been the assumption of most adults, and the mistaken inference has followed that, since there is no 'brain', nothing is needed save warmth and food. But there is awareness and memory even when there is as yet no organised self. Those who doubt this should read such studies as Dr. Partridge's little book, *The Baby's Point of View*, wherein is described the way in which the patient under analysis can recall the dreadful feeling of being bereft, even in the earliest days of life; or *The Origins of Love and Hate*, which illustrates how the early love relationship between mother and child determines the pattern and the possibility of all future loving. In the most utter and profound opposition to the Behaviourist school of Dr. J. B. Watson who severely deprecated any physical fondling of the infant, Dr. Suttie pleads for a total abolition of the 'taboo on tenderness' and on the physical demonstrations of tenderness which, he says, are as necessary to the child's well-being as is food for its body. The Puritanical attitude which frowns on expressions of tenderness causes 'a premature "psychic parturition" the damaging consequences of which may be life-long, and far more serious than those caused by any other taboo, such as that on sex. Indeed, the thwarting of sex is as nothing compared to the thwarting of infantile "love hunger", for in the too early separation from the mother's fondling the child is being deprived of something it has enjoyed from time immemorial, while in sexual repression it is merely being forbidden something that is reserved for grown-ups.'[2]

Obviously the love hunger and need of tenderness can only be satisfied at this early stage of life on the sensory plane through physical support, physical propinquity and physical endearments. Touch and bodily contact are far more fundamental sense experiences at the outset than sight or sound. 'Love' to the baby means tender feeling expressed in physical terms, and Suttie believed that the capacity for tenderness and affection in later life derived, not from sex desire, but 'from the pre-oedipal emotional and fondling relationship with the mother . . . which is characteristic of all animals that pass through a stage of nurtured infancy'.[3] (In this connection, it is interesting to note that in his study of the *Mentality of Apes* Koehler found that the chimpanzees could survive deprivation in the sphere of sex, but wilted and died if deprived of companionship—which he therefore inferred was a more fundamental need in them.)

It is of supreme importance, therefore, that the child's first symbiotic love relationship should not be damaged by what Dr. Kunkel calls a 'premature breach of the *we*', a too early psychic weaning, or the whole of his future development may suffer. The fact of separation from the mother's body in birth does not at all mean that the child is now ready to be away from his mother's body in the external world. Unlike the baby crocodile, the human infant has to build up a structure with which he can meet life and he cannot do this without constant, loving protection of his mother, or, at second best, his substitute mother. If denied this care, he becomes overwhelmed by terrors to an extent that the average adult cannot easily envisage. Thus follows the loss of the sense of security in love which lays the foundations for a general distrust of life and of one's fellows, and a turning outward to anti-social behaviour, or a turning inward to compensatory delusions—imagined phantasies of all that life has denied. Diagnosing such a condition with impressive names like 'paranoia' or 'melancholia' does not help the situation, or enable the poor victim to feel himself wanted and loved when he has already reached the conviction that all men are against him. It is a vicious circle, because self-pity, resentment and distrust of others are not qualities that win affection, and so, feeling himself unwanted and disliked, the sufferer sees here one further proof that all men save himself are bad. With such psychological casualties are the mental hospitals filled; of such are the alcoholics made; by such are crimes of hate, fear and jealousy committed; to such do avoidable accidents happen.

The famous Weir-Mitchell treatment went straight to the heart of the matter by providing the Baby-self in the adult sufferer with the environment appropriate to the infant: abundant food (the giving of food being a symbol to the child for the giving of love), silence, darkness, unbroken rest and unremitting attention. By saying to him in effect,

'This is what you really want, is it not?' the baby-self may be reassured by such care and attention, so long as the treatment lasts. The trouble generally starts when it ends, for the attention-hunger of the deprived person seems insatiable, and moving forward from the infantile level in adult life is a very much harder thing than is straightforward growth during infancy itself, where no fears, anxieties or love deprivations have blocked the normal process of development. A fractured limb may be restored without serious after-effects, but a fractured emotional life is never the same again. With the aid of long and loving patience, the emotional cripple may eventually come to do as well and as valiantly as does many a crippled body, but there is no place for easy optimism in this matter. Indeed, if the early damage was serious, the hope of recovery is correspondingly small. Studies have been carried out with delinquents and neurotics which show that psychiatric cure for those who experienced maternal rejection in infancy is practically impossible. John Bowlby tells us there are doctors who go so far as to assert that it is a waste of time attempting to cure those in whom no sort of love relationship was ever established in early infancy.

It may seem strange that the modern mother should be referred by the modern doctor to her more 'primitive' counterpart for lessons in the care of the young, yet in *The Lesson of Okinawa* we learn the surprising fact that the 'uneducated' people of that island have a better understanding of the infant's need of love and of close physical contact with the mother than does the average 'civilised' mother. It is the opinion of Dr. Moloney, President of the Michigan Society of Neurology and Psychiatry, that the psychological stamina of the Okinawan stems from the excellent start the child gets in life. He is well-mothered— that is to say, he is permitted the satisfaction of his normal cravings and instinctive needs during early life, and so is equipped with sufficient emotional stability to take later troubles in his stride. Dr. Moloney, who studied the

85

Okinawans at close range, says that 'a person not familiar with psychological maturative processes might be inclined to believe that the Okinawa brand of mothering would produce a self-centred, a spoiled, an undisciplined child. On the contrary, they show themselves capable of harmonious social co-operation. At Ishikawa I saw four thousand children performing collective drills, playing rather intricate group games. . . . There was not a single dissenter, not a single "problem child". Calm, confident, and without fear, they obeyed their elders, but were not obsequious. In following the games, they revealed a high degree of sportsmanship.[4]

The last thing I want to suggest is that the Okinawans or any other group of people have all the answers. Neither is Dr. Moloney suggesting that we all return to the comparatively smooth running of the undifferentiated tribe. Having broken away from that matrix, we must use our wits to think out the best way of doing things; we must look before and after and select consciously what was good in the past. If it is true that the Okinawan mother does a better job on the early emotional life of the child than does the more individuated and sophisticated, but also more anxious and intellectualised modern mother, the latter must learn to do consciously what the former does more or less unconsciously. But she must learn very much more than that, for when infancy is over each successive day of the child's life offers challenge to her wisdom. Many young couples embarking on marriage 'pooh-pooh' the difficulties. They are quite sure they will not repeat the mistakes of their parents. They are wiser and have the advantage of the latest research and have read all the latest books. But bringing up children is an art as well as a science; it requires that high degree of skill, delicacy of touch, sensitivity of feeling and keenness of insight that we associate with a very great artist in any sphere. These qualities cannot be acquired merely by study, though study has its place, and would have a very much larger place in a civilisation where such a stupendous event as the creation of a human being was taken seriously.

86

There are women who scorn child study, believing that their own 'instinct' will be adequate. But the fact that instinct seems to have functioned well in the comparatively simple society of Okinawa does not by any means prove that it can be relied upon as an infallible guide under all circumstances. For example, the Russian peasant woman, while giving admirable mothering in some respects, seems to fail deplorably in others, not from lack of love, but from lack of understanding. 'From the day of its birth onwards, the baby is tightly swaddled in long strips of material, holding its legs straight and its arms down by its sides. When Russians are asked why they swaddle their babies in this way, they give a considerable variety of reasons but they all have one common theme: the baby is potentially so strong that if it were not swaddled it would risk destroying itself or doing itself irreparable harm, and would be impossible to handle. For one mother, an unswaddled baby would risk developing a hunchback or crooked spine; others fear it would break its arms or legs or back by thrashing about, and would certainly have crooked limbs; others, again, that it would scratch out its eyes or ruin its nose. In the Ukraine in 1947, John Fischer was told by pediatricians, "If a baby's hands were left untrammelled, he would wave them in front of his face, thus getting a fright which might permanently upset the nervous system. All Russians are agreed that an unswaddled baby is impossible to handle, and would jump out of constraining arms. Russians exposed to Occidental practices justified swaddling on the ground that Russians had no perambulators."[5]

'When swaddled, the baby is completely rigid; one informant said the infants were like sticks. . . . The baby can be held in any position and by any part of it without bending. . . . The better the mother the firmer the bandages (the term which all my informants used for swaddling cloths). With a neat woman, the bandages would be harder, because she would have prepared in advance and made double layers of cloth and sewn them together. . . .[6]

For the possible effects of this treatment on the emotional life, the reader is referred to the psychological study, *The People of Great Russia*, by Gorer and Rickman. Some degree of swaddling has, of course, been practised in other parts of the world, notably in Italy and among the American Indians, but this extreme degree of constriction, combined with the habit of plugging the baby's mouth with a 'nib'—a ragful of chewed food—to stop its cries might well be part of the clue to the 'all-or-none' characteristic of the emotional reactions of the Russian adult. It is clear, therefore, that instinct alone is not a reliable guide, any more than intellect alone, in the nurturing of a child so that he will be capable of creative loving and living.

Man has been given this strange and yet priceless gift of a long period of helplessness in which he remains supple and immature so that by exploring life for himself, he may learn how to learn and become a human being instead of an ant, bee or fascist. A chicken is 'better off' than a baby because it is fully equipped to satisfy all its needs from the start, only a chicken will be no wiser at the end of its life. It is man's helplessness that makes mental development possible for him, but it also leaves him utterly at the mercy of those around him. If they fail him in affectionate companionship, if they become impatient with his long dependence, do not give him time to develop at his own rate, but impose their arbitrary standards under the euphemism of 'training' before the child is ready for them, then how can he fail to develop deep anxieties, fears and duplicities which will shadow all his life and make free and joyous loving impossible?

It is not, of course, being suggested that children can only receive psychological damage in early infancy. Current literature is all too full of illustrations of the damage that can take place in schooldays, even in what are supposedly religious schools. For example, a mother of limited ideas was over-concerned that her son should grow up into 'a good man'. Therefore at the tender age of eight, she sent him away to a choristers' school because there he would attend the Cathedral services twice a day and that could not fail to have a beneficial and lifelong influence on him. What actually influenced him was something very different and was unguessed at by his non-perceptive mother. He heard all the words about love and goodness in the daily services, but in school he had the misfortune to learn to fear, and consequently to hate. His trust in people being undermined, he lost the capacity for spontaneous response to life. The baleful influences easily triumphed over the verbal, because, as we have seen, what we experience through our feelings is infinitely more potent than what we learn from the spoken word. Such damage is not necessarily irreparable; healing and re-creation may come with a new environment of loving-kindness and understanding. But the severity of the damage will be very largely determined by the wholesomeness of the child's earliest relationship with his mother; on whether the foundations of a loving nature were well and truly laid at the start.

And if it is asked, 'But what has this to do with religion?' the answer is: 'Everything.' If God is Love, then it follows that love is the heart of all religious experience and that a man unable to bestow or to win affection is an irreligious man. 'But', it may be questioned, 'cannot a man learn to love if he will?' No; not necessarily, and not unless he receives a great deal of help. We have already seen that a child who has been made fearful and unstable in infancy is likely to become a fearful, unstable and resentful adult, too deeply occupied in seeking for that protective loving care he missed to have any thoughtful concern for others.

The alarming anxiety and insecurity in the soul of man to-day is traceable at least in part to the fact that mothers may be too unimaginative, or too self-centred, or just too plain 'busy' to give the child the love he so desperately needs, especially in infancy. It cannot be repeated too often that unless psychological health is reasonably well established in the early years, then in later life there can be no genuine love life and consequently no religious life. Therefore the pastor who preaches the duty of loving should stress the damage that can be done to the capacity for love through failure to see that the child is 'well-mothered', otherwise he may be wasting his time. For while to a loving nature the exhortation to love is superfluous, to an unloved one it is futile.

It is necessary to stress this one aspect of early love because it has received too little attention in the past, and because modern explorations into the unconscious have demonstrated its immense importance. But it would be an error to suggest that all problems of human relationships would be solved if only children were well-mothered in infancy. Life is never that simple. Neither must it be deduced that loving means continuous coddling at the expense of character development. One can 'spoil' a child in different ways. Over-indulgence, protracting infantile dependence unduly is one way; forcing the pace is another. If in our anxiety to produce well-behaved, rock-ribbed characters, we give children more difficulty than, in their immaturity, they are capable of meeting, then we defeat our own ends and produce, instead of the perfection we planned, unstable and resentful rather than loving and generous-hearted adults.

Wise loving is not easy, not something with which motherhood is automatically endowed, as the sentimentalist likes to think. Loving means not merely to care for and have nice feelings about, but to respect, to be tolerant, to be firm on occasion, and always to try to understand. Positive loving, as distinct from easy emotionalism, is hard work. Knowledge of child psychology is of value when wisely applied, but the application requires alert intuition and keen sensitivity. The psychologist may advise the mother to do this or that, to follow the laws of the child's being, and to avoid extremes; to give him enough difficulty at each stage of development to challenge without depressing him, enough conflict to strengthen his judgement and his moral fibre without unduly discouraging him, enough structure for guidance without rigidity, enough freedom for expression without swinging too wide into licence, and always enough encouragement and approval to stimulate further effort. But who knows what is 'enough'? There is not and never could be a book giving detailed rules and exact answers. Each incident must be judged by itself in the light of the total context, not by reference to some external authority. It is a matter of keeping a fine balance, of walking a razor's edge. It is 'the artist's secret', and therefore he is no educator who is not in his degree a creative artist in living.

But lest the task of child nurture has now been made to sound altogether too difficult for any ordinary individual to undertake, lest the suggestion has been conveyed that anything short of perfection in the handling of young children would be disastrous, let the parent or teacher be reassured with the words of St. Augustine: 'Love, and do what you will.' Some mistakes are inevitable, and it is better to go ahead and risk a mistake than live in an atmosphere of tension and anxiety as to whether one is doing the right thing. Children can forgive, and survive, quite a large amount of questionable handling provided they feel themselves to be wanted and sincerely loved by mutually loving parents.

CHAPTER V

EXPERIENCE OF BEAUTY: ITS RELATION TO RELIGION

When we see supreme beauty, either in nature or in art, we do not—we cannot—ask, of what use is it? What could it do for me? or How much does it demand of me? As Manet said, 'We stand moved', we are arrested, rapt, altered. In our unguarded self-forgetfulness we 'give ourselves away.' The consciousness which catches sight of beauty, which is caught up by loveliness, is instantly and purely brought into an act of worship.

GERALD HEARD: *A Preface to Prayer.*

IS THE EXPERIENCE of beauty an essential part of the religious life? Is the appreciation and creation of beauty an essential part of education? The Puritans did not think so, and their influence has done much to discredit love of the beautiful right up to our own times. A story written by Maria Edgeworth in the nineteenth century illustrates this fact—the story of Rosamund and the purple jar. Rosamund's mother had promised to give her a present. Privately the mother intended it to take the form of a pair of shoes, but she gave her daughter the appearance of choice. Rosamund had developed a passionate longing for one of the large, gleaming, coloured jars that she saw whenever she passed the window of the chemist's shop. Her mother decided she needed a lesson, so she allowed Rosamund to have the jar but did not tell her that the colour was in the liquid, not in the glass. When it arrived home the poor child found herself the owner of a large, colourless glass jar and no new shoes in which to go to her party. The moral of the tale was that utility is a higher good than beauty, and that the best way for Rosamund to learn this was through experience, however bitter.

We need not doubt that the mother was a kindly woman according to her lights, but from the aesthetic point of view her sense of values was strictly limited. That they were the accepted values of her day is illustrated by a contemporary couplet:

'I slept and dreamed that life was beauty.
I woke, and found that life was duty.'

The implication is that, beauty and duty being incompatible, one must choose between them. To-day we no longer believe this is true; on the contrary, we believe that the mother who plays with her children at making 'rainbows' with a glass on the floor of a sunny room, or the father who takes them out in the early morning to see the bejewelled spider webs or at night to watch the moths and the glow worms—these parents are not failing in, but fulfilling their duty.

During a recent discussion on the sorry state of mankind, the question was asked, 'Is anything taking place in the schools which might give ground for hope?' One answer given was that the great change which shifted the centre of interest from the curriculum to the child is still in process of consummation. Another more recent change bringing fresh hope in our own day, is the dawning realisation that beauty is a fundamental value which exists in its own right, a thing to be appreciated and expressed in joyous creativity, not a frill to be tacked on to an otherwise serious curriculum; not a means to some other useful end, like passing an examination or earning a living.

In the early twentieth century, the arts were not neglected, but in many schools they had no relation to beauty and were treated almost wholly as a discipline. Music, drawing, literature were compulsory subjects and were emotionally

93

toned with dreariness and apprehension rather than with creative joy. Marks were given for accuracy of reproduction and efficiency of performance; prizes were given for examinations successfully passed; but there was no hint that every beautiful finite thing is a window by which the soul may catch a glimpse of the infinite.

Into such an orthodox classroom, an imaginative teacher once appeared at the beginning of the century. She told the children to select a poem to learn by heart, and to give reasons for their choice. They were bewildered, and floundered as helplessly as fish on dry land. They did not know how to function in such a medium of free choice, for they had always been given to understand that it was not for them to have likes and dislikes, but obediently to learn or copy whatever authority directed. The criterion of merit was accuracy of reproduction and skill in performance. That one might enjoy a drawing lesson or a music lesson never entered the consciousness either of teacher or taught, and would have created a sense of guilt if it had.

The pendulum has swung with a vengeance. Instead of telling the child what to draw, we now hesitate to ask the child to tell us what he has drawn. We certainly would not presume to try to improve his work, for while he is still a child we realise that his feelings and his own unhampered expression of them are more important than techniques. We have become more concerned that he should perceive beauty for himself than that he should make an accurate reproduction of something we think has beauty.

Therefore, while sharing Freya Stark's regret that beauty should still be 'so little cared for in our schools',[1] one may yet maintain that it is gradually achieving a higher status and that there has been a fundamental change of attitude in the teaching of art as such. This change is in part due to the realisation that successful development requires that we function with our total selves, head, heart and hand in collaboration, not with any one in isolation from the rest.

94

Needless to say, this revolution of attitude is not yet universal. There still exist nursery schools in California where art work starts for babes of three with 'learning the principles of colour and design' and 'progressive education' is regarded as 'so much hog-wash'. But among *bona-fide* educators there is unquestioning acceptance of the principle that experience must precede theory, and that unless the intellect is fed from the springs of feeling it is in danger of becoming amputated, as it were, from life.

To cut children off from their feelings in the name of education is as disastrous as to cut them off from all contact with the beauty of the earth. In both cases their souls will as surely suffer a deficiency disease as would their bodies if fed on a vitaminless diet. A young student teacher once arranged for a group of city children to visit a large country garden outside London. From a mistaken sense of duty, not having yet outgrown the notion that the real function of a teacher is to administer verbal instructions, she had planned to teach the names of birds, trees and flowers, so that the expedition would not be 'wasted'. The children, however, had other ideas. They came to a grassy bank, and proceeded to roll down it in a state of ecstasy for the entire afternoon. It was their first experience of close contact with the earth, and, like babes long separated from their 'mother', it seemed they could not now get enough of her. Older children, taken for the first time from the East End into the country, have been known to stroke the green grass in loving wonder, finding it—

'Soft as the breast of doves
And shivering sweet to the touch.'[2]

Such experience is the child's birthright and is as necessary to his spiritual health as is parental love. It is related that a Buddhist monk once took a flower and placed it in silence before his congregation, and that was all his sermon. Jesus preached a similar sermon: 'Consider the lilies.' But if the

95

only flowers a child ever sees are those on the dingy wall-paper of a city dwelling, then we deprive him of the opportunity of finding God in the beauty of the earth. The author of *The Will of a Lunatic* was wiser than most men when he bequeathed to children 'the banks of the brooks and the golden sands beneath the waters thereof, and the odours of the willows that dip therein, and the white clouds that float high over giant trees . . . and the night and the train of the Milky Way to wonder at . . . and all clover meadows with the clover blossoms and butterflies thereof; the woods with their beauty; the squirrels and the birds and the echoes and strange noises; and all distant places which may be visited, together with the adventures there found.'

A child who has deeply participated in these delights in early life can never thereafter suffer complete disillusionment, can never wholly lose faith in life, even if he loses anchorage in his dogmatic religion or confidence in his fellow men. But a city child, cut off from all contact with his mother earth and with the world of nature, should be classified as 'underprivileged' no matter what his social status. The English boy of seven who, on seeing New York for the first time, asked, 'But where are the gardens, and where do people dig?' realised at once that something essential was missing and had been left out of account in that great city. There is a similar story of a Japanese girl who, confronted by the crowded city slum dwellings from an English railway train, burst into tears and cried, 'These people have no view.'

As for the connection between aesthetic and religious experience, it is impossible to state where one ends and the other begins. They are not identical, but they appear to lie on the same continuum, the one leading naturally to the other. 'Beauty', says Plotinus, 'is always a trace of the divine.' Yet the analytic mind can so easily cause a rift which severs the connection between them, and, as Aldous Huxley points out, the failure to relate oneself to the Whole can increase that rift. 'If the poet remains content with his

96

gift (a great and precious gift), if he persists in worshipping the beauty in art and nature without going on to make himself capable, through selflessness, of apprehending Beauty as it is in the Divine Ground, then he is only an idolater. True, his idolatry is among the highest of which human beings are capable; but an idolatry, none the less, it remains.'[3]

In young children, however, before the intellect has made those inevitable but artificial separations which hinder the perception of wholeness, aesthetic experience and mystic experience may be known as one event. The child does not have to make himself 'capable . . . of apprehending Beauty as it is in the Divine Ground'; he is already capable; the keen awareness of the beautiful itself constitutes for him a theophany. As one mystic put it: 'Certainly Adam in Paradise had not more sweet and curious apprehensions of the world than I when I was a child.'

Children capable of such experience seldom mention it at the time. It would be difficult to express in words, and in any case it is accepted as quite natural, as part of the total wonder of life. The following examples have been recalled and described by various individuals in their maturity:

'The thing happened one summer afternoon, on the school cricket field, while I was sitting on the grass, waiting for my turn to bat. I was thinking about nothing in particular merely enjoying the pleasures of midsummer idleness. Suddenly and without warning, something invisible seemed to be drawn across the sky, transforming the world around me into a kind of tent of concentrated and enhanced significance. What had been merely outside became an inside. The objective was somehow transformed into a completely subjective fact, which was experienced as "mine", but on a level where that word had no meaning; for "I" was no longer the familiar ego. Nothing more can be said about the experience; for though it was cognitive, it brought no accession of knowledge about anything except, very obscurely, the knower and his way of knowing. After a few minutes there was a "return to normalcy". The event made a very deep impression on me at the time; but, because it did not fit into any of the thought patterns—religious, philosophical, scientific—with which, as a boy of fifteen, I was familiar, it came to seem more and more anomalous, more and more irrelevant to "real life", and was finally almost forgotten.'

Another example comes from an elderly woman who recalls how, as a child of nine, she was given charge of her baby sister one Sunday afternoon and told she could take her into the meadows which she loved. 'I took off my shoes and stockings, carried the baby across the stream, and laid her down gently under the lime trees, which were in bloom and smelling most beautifully. There were soft white clouds in the sky, but the sun was shining. Everything was very quiet save for the munching of the lazy, melancholy cows, and the gentle burble of the brook, whose banks were covered with lacy meadow-sweet, pink willow-herb, and sky-blue forget-me-nots. Suddenly the Thing happened, and, as everybody knows, it cannot be described in words. The Bible phrase "I saw the heavens open" seems as good as any if it is not taken literally. I remember saying to myself, in awe and rapture, "So it's like this: now I know what Heaven is like, now I know what they mean in church." The words of the 23rd Psalm came into my head and I began repeating them: "He maketh me lie down in green pastures; he leadeth me beside the still waters." Soon It faded and I was alone in the meadow with the baby and the brook and the sweet-smelling lime trees. But although it had passed and only the earthly beauty remained, I was filled with a great gladness; I had seen the "far distances".'

Another woman writes: 'From time to time during my childhood I was visited by "intimations" from the Beyond. Once as I was walking along a sandy lane in autumn, I saw a yellow maple bush caught by the slanting evening sunlight and "afire with God"; and once when I was sitting in the fork of an old apple tree in our garden, gazing through its tender blossoms to the blue sky above, I saw through to "the other side".' Yet another recalls how 'as a child, when walking home along the country road after Evensong, my father carrying a candle-lantern to light our way, I would look up into the starry heavens and experience an intensity of awe and wonder that seemed to take me right out of my body. I never mentioned these moments of ecstasy, for life was bringing them continuously in some form and degree, such as the coming of daffodils in spring, the falling of snow, or the sound of the waves. Moreover, I took it for granted that everyone felt the same. In later life I realised I had lost this capacity to see and to feel. I tried hard to recapture it by conscious willing, but I never could. It had faded into the light of common day. The world was still beautiful, but the Vision Splendid was not there. Yet the memory of the childhood vision has remained with me vividly through the years, and to-day strengthens my conviction that this life which we normally know through our senses is not the whole life, but that "somewhere beyond these earthly shadows, there is a world of light eternal".'

This fading of the capacity for vision with the passing of childhood appears to be a common experience, and some seem to forget that they ever had it—if indeed they did. 'Four-year-old Bobby, in the enthusiasm of his first experience, corralled all the family on the front porch to see the sunset. When ten-year-old Ned came, however, he looked around a moment and said casually, "Oh, its only the horizon, and it's been there for years." Then he returned to his own game.'4 More often, however, the memory remains, and sometimes it becomes more conscious and meaningful, as the following example illustrates: 'I must have been between five and six when this experience happened to me. It was a summer morning, and the child I was had walked down through the orchard alone and come out on the brow of a sloping hill where there was grass and a wind blowing and one tall tree reaching into infinite immensities of blueness. Quite suddenly, after a moment of

99

quietness there, earth and sky and tree and wind-blown grass and the child in the midst of them came alive together with a pulsing light of consciousness. There was a wild foxglove at the child's feet and a bee dozing about it, and to this day I can recall the swift, inclusive awareness of each for the whole. I in them and they in me and all of us enclosed in a warm, lucent bubble of livingness. I remember the child looking everywhere for the source of this happy wonder, and at last she questioned—God?—because it was the only awesome word she knew. Deep inside, like the murmurous swinging of a bell, she heard the answer, "God, God. . . ."

'How long this ineffable moment lasted I never knew. It broke like a bubble at the sudden singing of a bird, and the wind blew and the world was the same as ever—only never quite the same. The experience so initiated has been the one abiding reality of my life, unalterable except in the abounding fulness and frequency of its occurrence.'[5]

These mystic experiences of childhood were all associated with the beauty of the earth. This is not surprising when nature is 'the Vicaire of th' Almighty Lord'.[6] But nature is not the only 'Vicaire'. For those with ears to hear and eyes to see, there are around us beauties in endless patterns of sight, sound, movement and form, and to these, individuals will vary both in sensitivity of response and in the aspect of beauty to which they are most receptive. Quite young children can be stirred by the beauty of words and sentences, without necessarily understanding their meaning. But great literature can be ruined if read without feeling or rhythm. Mary Webb describes for us her reaction to the murderous reading of the Lessons: 'It always werrited me in church when sexton read out of the Bible, for no matter what he read, it all sounded like a bee in a bottle. It didna matter when he was reading "And he took unto him a wife and begat Aminadab" . . . for it was naught to me if he did. But when there were things to be read with a sound in 'em like the wind in the aspen tree, it seemed a pitiful thing that he should mouth it over so. . . . I wanted to be able to read "Or ever the silver cord be loosed" for myself, and savour it.'[7]

Revelation can come too through beauty of form. Richard Hertz tells how in his youth religion meant nothing to him save 'another bulging telephone directory' until he saw the Cathedral of Chartres. 'Indeed', he says, 'Chartres was the greatest lesson I received in my life.'[8] He was not alone in this experience.

There are also subtle forms of beauty which are supreme in their own right, but which tend so often to be overlooked, either because we are unpractised in seeing or because they are less obvious. Plotinus saw the face of Justice and Wisdom as 'Beautiful beyond the beauty of the evening star or the dawn'. And in our own day other philosophers penetrated these mysteries with the same insight. Whitehead writes: 'Of all manifestations of life, virtue is the most beautiful.'[9] Niebuhr expands the same thought as follows: 'There is another kind of beauty I faintly glimpse that isn't just the sweet smells and lovely sights and harmonious lines; it's the beauty that can't endure disharmony in conduct, the fine, true ear for the loveliness of life lived at its best.'

In this connection, Niebuhr argues that the qualities of harmony and proportion, of grace and nobility of movement and form, all of which we should have in mind when judging a picture, can also be our criteria when judging human lives, where their absence is even more serious than on canvas. 'Perhaps our race', he writes, 'not specially inspired for its instinct for colour and external form, may possibly be fumbling towards an art of living. Why wouldn't it be an art to keep your life in drawing as well as a mural decoration? The technique would be quite as difficult to acquire. . . . Isn't there a beauty as a possible ideal of aspiration for a race that probably never could achieve a Florentine or Japanese beauty of line?'[10]

The final thing to be considered about beauty is its relation to truth. It would seem that they cannot be separated, that without beauty, truth is at best non-significant and at worst harmful; that mere truth of fact unrelated to truth of value may result in evil. The discovery of scientific truths such as those that have given us our new mastery over nuclear fission, drives us like Gadarene swine down the steep hill to our doom, unless it is related to a positive conception of the unity of all things in their right relationship, the unity for which the artist in each one of us is always striving.

The realisation of this danger caused Anatole France to write that if he had to choose between truth and beauty he would not hesitate to retain beauty, 'confident that it embodies a higher and profounder truth than truth itself'. However, if Keats is right, he would never have to choose between them since, in the last resort,

'Beauty is truth, truth beauty'.

CHAPTER VI

EXPERIENCE OF JOY AND PAIN:
THEIR RELATION TO EACH OTHER

I. Sampler worked by Susannah Catherine Ward, aged nine, 1791

Let children that would fear the Lord
Hear what their teachers say;
With reverence meet their parents' word
And with delight obey.

Have you not heard what dreadful plagues
Are threatened by the Lord
To him that breaks his father's law,
Or mocks his mother's word?

What heavy guilt upon him lies,
How cursed is his name.
The ravens shall pick out his eyes
And eagles eat the same.

But those who worship God, and give
Their parents honour due,
Here on this earth they long shall live,
And live hereafter too.

II. Poem composed by Anne Curry, aged ten, 1940

THINGS I LOVE

The blue sky above,
The coo of a dove,
Spring flowers in bloom,
Daffodils in a room.

103

To swim in the sea
And ride my pony,
To canter along
And hear the wind's song.

To skate on the ice
Is very nice,
To play in the snow
And see my sledge go!

To feel the sun warm
And watch shadows form.
To lie on the sand
In dear England.

LIKE 'BEAUTY', the concepts of joy, happiness, pleasure and all associated words are still a trifle suspect to those of us in the West who were brought up in an atmosphere not yet freed from the Puritanical and Patriarchal tradition. When a famous evangelistic preacher required his coachman to 'Go and tell those children to stop playing and contemplate their eternal welfare', the order caused no surprise, for not only were the offending children blasphemously disporting among the tombstones; they were wasting time; worse still, they were happy, and happiness was not for this world.

'There is a happy land
Far, far away',

said the contemporary hymn, and it might be you would never get there if you dared to enjoy life here.

'Here we suffer grief and pain.'

It was better to accept the fact and not get your parts confused, but to decide boldly between the clear-cut and stupendous alternatives:

'To inherit bliss unending
Or eternity of woe.'

The two children's poems that head this chapter illustrate
the enormous change of attitude that has come about in our
educational theory and practice, largely as a result of
Froebel's insight into 'the high meaning in childish play'.
The eighteenth-century child dutifully and mechanically
stitched out the repressive and dreary sentiments of her
elders: the modern child, though uprooted from her home
by war, spontaneously expresses her joy in life. The sampler
used the language of religion, but is in reality blasphemous:
the second poem does not mention God or Heaven, but
has in it all the elements of true religious feeling; as had
the small child who, when asked by her mother, 'Why
are you so excited, Olivia?' replied, '*Maman, je suis excitée
de vivre.*' A young teacher, singing joyously to herself in
the playground, was accosted by a small boy with the
surprised comment: 'You're happy, aren't you, miss?' He
evidently found it unusual for a grown-up to be happy
enough to sing, and one must admit he was right: it is
unusual.

And yet Tagore tells us, 'Only he has achieved final
truth who knows that the whole universe is a creation of
joy.' If that is so, it follows that a joyless person is not a
very religious person, for he is missing a fundamental truth
about life, and, no matter what his beliefs, he is less in
touch with the heart of reality than a child dancing in the
meadows.

'We want you to keep your "vital feelings of delight",
your "sweet and curious apprehensions of the world" '[1] was
one mother's prayer for her child—a religious prayer,
because without such feelings of delight reality cannot be
known or appreciated. One wonders at the nature of the
spiritual sickness that insisted on children dwelling exclusively on the pain and sadness of life. Even at the tender
age of seven, a child asked in her embroidery:

'Lord what is life? 'Tis like a flower
      That blossoms and is gone.
We see it flourish for an hour
      With all its beauty on.
But death comes like a wintry day
And cuts the pretty flower away.'

True enough, but hardly a wholesome diet for children,
and not comparable to the contemporary hymn:

'Glad that I live am I,
      That the sky is blue;
Glad for the country lanes,
      And the fall of dew.'

Must we choose between these two attitudes? Must we
decide to be either joyous *or* sad? Must we encourage our
children to adopt *either* the 'Vale of Tears' outlook *or* 'The
Right to Happiness' as a philosophy? No; we cannot if we
would so choose, since both joy and woe are intrinsic to life.
To try to ignore either the one or the other would therefore
be as foolish as Canute's attempt to stop the ebb and flow
of the tides, or as to try inhaling without exhaling. The
choice before us is not whether we will take gladness or
sadness as our goal, but whether we will take both as and
when they come, and use both as a means of reaching out
towards the larger goal of growth and development.

In similar vein, Shakespeare speaks to us through Hamlet:

'For thou hast been
As one, in suffering all, that suffers nothing,
A man that fortune's buffets and rewards
      Hast ta'en with equal thanks; and blest are those
Whose blood and judgment are so well commingled
That they are not a pipe for Fortune's finger
To sound what stop she please.'

106

So the creative spirit will go on learning what it can through all that may happen, be it joyous or grievous.

The truth is not necessarily the opposite of the false; it is sometimes to be found in another realm which includes the opposites but transcends them. Expressed in Hegel's familiar concept, the triad of thesis, antithesis and synthesis, we should then have:

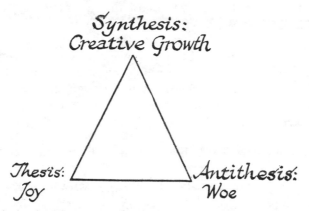

This is the answer to both Puritan and Hedonist; to the person who believes in 'discipline' and to the one who believes in 'having a good time'. Both see a part of the truth which they mistake for the whole. The modern expression of the latter attitude takes such forms as: 'I want my children to be happy; they'll have enough misery and hardship to face later on; let them enjoy themselves while they can.' The disciplinarian on the other hand asks: 'How can so much freedom to do what they please prepare children for life? They are getting wrong ideas. Life isn't like that and they'll get an awful shock when they go out into the world.'

In neither case is the answer simply 'Yes' or 'No'. The answer remains a question: 'Are these children growing on every plane of their being? Are they developing to the utmost of their power all their potentialities in the realms of body, mind and spirit? Are they learning both to love life *and* to accept its inevitable deprivations; to rejoice, and also to suffer with courage when suffering, which is inevitable in the world as we know it, must be their portion?

The test of willingness to learn is the only true test of whether or not education is on the right lines and is being conducted according to the first law of life, the law of growth. If it is, then children will be basically happy because happiness is a natural concomitant of development and of the unfolding of one's powers.

The word 'unfolding' must not mislead us into thinking that the unfolding of human powers can be entirely the same effortless thing as the unfolding of a flower or a tree, for human nature is something more complex than either. It is indeed the most complex form of life we know. Browning sang truly:

> 'How good is man's life, the mere living, how fit to
>   employ
> Both the heart and the soul and the senses, forever in
>   joy.'

Yes; but 'Decay, Transition, Loss, Displaccmcnt, also belong to the essence of the creative advance',[2] and the more highly developed the consciousness, the greater its imaginative power, and therefore the greater its capacity to create and to suffer. If we try, like the followers of certain questionable modern religions and philosophies, to have it all one way, and to escape from pain by denying that it exists, then we shall not develop our understanding. The same Jesus who said, 'These things have I spoken unto you, that My joy might remain in you, and that your joy might be full,' also said, 'Whosoever will come after Me, let him deny himself and take up his cross.'

What is called 'the principle of the opposites' appears to run through all life. Blake tells us: 'Life was made for joy and woe.' Whether it was or not, joy and woe are there as inevitably as light and dark, good and evil, love and hate, beauty and ugliness. If we overprotect children from the dark side of these opposites, we do them a disservice. For later, when the inevitable awakening comes, they may suffer a severe shock, like the overprotected Gautama Buddha; or they may feel resentment against their too kindly guardians and demand: 'Why did you mislead us? Why did you not tell us what life was really like!' Baron von Hugel was wiser when he wrote to his beloved niece: 'I want to prepare you, to organise you for life, for illness, crisis or death. Live all you can, as complete and full a life as you can find; do as much as you can for others. Read, work, enjoy . . . do all this, yes, but remember: be alone, be remote, be desolate. Then you will be near God.'

Plato may or may not have been wrong in his assertion: 'Evil, Theodorus, can never pass away.' How would one know? But at least he was no more wrong than the pseudo-'religions' of to-day that turn their backs on the reality of evil, urging us to stop worrying and just float, relying on God's goodness and loving-kindness. The emotional attitude of the trusting child is a good attitude for a child to have, but those capable of growth must not be brought up in blinkers. Life includes the experience of '*de profundis*' as well as of '*Jubilate deo*'. Spiritual maturity necessitates a deeper descent if the ascent is to be higher; the exploration of the vertical as well as of the horizontal dimension:

> 'I made thee three in one and one in three—
> Spirit and Mind and Form, immortal Whole,
> Divine and undivided Trinity.'[3]

When these three interact as they should, so that—

> 'Mind sees by spirit; Body moves by Mind.'[4]

then life may be fundamentally happy even though its rhythm includes struggle and suffering.

Therefore in an education that is truthfully related to all

of life, the goal should be not to 'make children happy', but to see to it that they have opportunity for the development of their powers in every direction, so that they may know not only the happiness that accompanies creative and productive activity, but also the hard effort and even the suffering that will at times be involved in the process.

This is a stern as well as a joyous gospel, and the lazy part of us does not welcome the sternness in it. The unconscious mind has therefore produced the myth of the Garden of Eden which expresses both our nostalgic hunger for the Golden Age of infancy and also our detestation for the 'curse' of toil. We long to flee this life of care and get back to the peace of the Garden—that is, to the care-free innocence of childhood, where the only requirement was obedience. But we cannot, for there at the gates stand the cherubim with the flaming sword, and the relentless judgement, 'In the sweat of thy brow shalt thou eat bread' and its implicit threat that 'If a man will not work, neither shall he eat'.

In psychological terms, this myth implies that we must grow up and shoulder the responsibilities of life, or pay the price that inevitably follows retreat—the price, namely, of blocked development, perhaps taking the form of some mental illness that draws the mind backwards instead of forwards. The backward pull is understandable enough in view of the fact that every increase in conscious awareness spells for us a corresponding increase in anxiety with fresh responsibilities to be faced and fresh burdens to be carried; not only for ourselves, but, as our imagination widens and our capacity for love deepens, for others also. The burden may at times seem intolerable, and the longing for the peace of the lost Garden overwhelming; but if, like Lot's wife, we succumb to this nostalgia, then we shall meet the fate of Lot's wife. The directive is absolute: Go forward, or become a pillar of dead matter from which the spirit has fled.

This ultimatum is not very pleasant, especially as it is interpreted by the infant mind in us to be punitive. Superficially we may accept the punishment as just, knowing that at some time or other we have disobeyed our parents and that disobedience is 'sin' and that sin deserves punishment. Thus do we try to get rid of our guilty feelings. But in the unconscious the situation is not so readily accepted and may produce a bitter resentment which expresses itself in a mixture of 'sour grapes' and of cruelty: 'if happiness is denied me because of my "sin", then happiness in this life is wrong. But since I can't be happy, I'll see to it that you are not.' The miscalled Puritan then proceeds to 'purify'—that is, to destroy—the things that bring happiness to others, the things non-Puritans appear to value most.

A further disaster, due at least in part to this unconscious split in the mind, is the artificial division of life's activities, once regarded merely as activities, into those called work, now put under a curse and therefore inevitably unpleasant, and those called play which are a waste of time and only to be tolerated in the useless period of infancy until proper and profitable occupation can be undertaken. On one day of the week all activity of any sort is evil and a blasphemy against God:

'I must not work, I must not play
Upon God's holy Sabbath day,'

though one might go to Church and hear it announced that 'The Sabbath was made for man and not man for the sabbath'.

To-day Puritanism, though still with us, has become sufficiently flexible to admit the advisability of some form of relaxation for the individual who has finished his daily work. He may, to the exclusion of certain activities which are regarded as evil in themselves, such as card games, horse-racing or drinking alcoholic liquor, be allowed to enjoy himself in any way that he pleases, trivial or creative. Unfortunately, since the division has been made in that which was once organically related, play for the majority degenerated into some mainly passive form of entertainment which makes no demands for participation beyond the price of a ticket, and work is the serious but so often tiresome activity by which we earn a living. Both are regarded as secular and as having no connection with things sacred and holy, which are restricted to specific times and places.

It is said to be hard for Eastern philosophy to comprehend this dissociation between religious and secular in music, in the arts and in our daily life. It would have been equally hard for ancient Greece in its best period before the sense of the interrelatedness of all things was lost. The Greeks once regarded their play—athletics, drama, music, etc.—as part of their religious life, and the great tragedians wrote their 'plays' around religious topics which were concerned with man's relation to the Universe. This sense of wholeness was largely lost after the devastating wars of the fifth century B.C., and the theatre, which had once been a kind of temple, degenerated first into a place of entertainment by conjurors and sword-swallowers, and then later into a place of gladiatorial combats.

We must now try to recover this lost sense of wholeness, to do consciously what the Greeks once did naturally: to eat and drink, to practise the arts or politics or whatsoever we do, 'to the glory of God'. 'I most potently believe', wrote Lowes Dickenson, 'that unless and until the art of politics is brought into touch with the spiritual life, it will remain what it has always been, barren and fruitless. . . . Sages arise continually with the same message. Until that is accepted, we shall not progress; we shall fluctuate. For our passions, our intellects, and our spirits are in unstable equilibrium; and until we connect the spiritual life with the political . . . both will remain paralysed.'[5]

It is useless to indulge in nostalgia for the past, whether 'the glory that was Greece' or the 'Golden Age' of early childhood, when work was play and play was work. What we have to do now is to move forward and consciously try to heal the breach between the two at a new level. Occasionally we see an example of this healing harmony as in the case of the young teacher singing at her work. Occasionally we hear someone make the refreshing remark, 'I love my work'—and many would add: 'I should love mine too if it was not overwork'.

Overwork is, like overplay, a mistake, but the essential difference between work and play is not a matter of ease *versus* hardship as the Puritan and the 'waster' minds both think. It is a matter of following one's inner urge to write, to carve, to go into politics, to farm, or to go exploring, because one wants to, because one feels fulfilled and happily related to life and of service to life, through this particular activity.

This is, of course, a utopian ideal in the world as it is. Many people have little if any creative urge; many others who have are obliged to forgo its expression. But much of the tedium of uncongenial work is lifted when it is done for love, and more still when it is done *ad majorem gloriam dei*. For if George Herbert was right—

> 'This is the famous stone
> That turneth all to gold.'

and makes 'drudgery divine'.

But even on the plane of this world, and when the urge is strong, it is astonishing how much 'work', effort and hardship is cheerfully undertaken because of the interest in the goal. If the mountaineers who have periodically assaulted Mt. Everest had been forced into this activity by some sadistic dictator, what a cruel task it would have seemed.

Of the ill-fated expedition to the South Pole, Captain Scott wrote in his diary a few days before the end: 'We are in a very tight place indeed, but none of us is despondent yet, or at least we preserve every semblance of good cheer.' They were all suffering terribly and knew that the chance of coming through was negligible, yet (referring to Captain Oates), 'We all hope to meet the end in a similar spirit'.

It was their 'determined good cheer' in the midst of their desperate circumstances that stirred the heart of the world and gave a new meaning to gallantry. The fact that their enterprise 'failed' is, from this angle, irrelevant. They triumphed as human beings and bore witness to the potential grandeur of the spirit of man.

This same spirit spoke also through Alfred, the great king, who, when the Danes laughed at his pitiful, ragged army, replied:

'That though we scatter and though we fly
And you hang over us like the sky,
You are more tired of victory
    Than we are tired of shame.

'That though you hunt the Christian man
Like a hare on the hill side,
The hare has still more heart to run
    Than you have heart to ride.

'That though all lances split on you
All swords be heaved in vain,
We have more lust again to lose
    Than you to win again.'[6]

It is to such men that our deepest admiration goes, those who enterprise in the realm of spirit, not merely in the conquest of the globe. Unfortunately, the word 'enterprise' is now so closely associated with business and industry that we tend to overlook its more important expressions, which take men forward in an inwardly significant sense. Yet it is these whose names survive the test of time; it is these who lift up our hearts in joy and hope, for they tell us what in our deepest selves we want most of all to hear: that more is in us, and more is possible for us than we dream of, if we will have the enterprise to send our souls adventuring:

'Fearless, for unknown shores,
On waves of ecstasy to sail.'

114

The Puritan resents the suffering in the journey, and so consoles and perhaps enjoys himself by seeing to it that others shall not be happy. The waster and the escapist refuse the suffering and try to turn back to the Eden of their infancy. The mental homes are full of such unwilling pilgrims. The world's great fairy tales, embodying as they do the unconscious wisdom of the ages, do not describe man as finding his happiness in comfort, security or escape. The triumphant heroes are neither the protected nor the embittered, but those who, facing great peril, yet go forth to meet and slay the dragon. They are always presented as battling mightily against evil before they come into their kingdom and receive their reward. The originators of these stories knew in some deep, intuitive way that suffering and happiness are intertwined, that

> Joy and woe are woven fine,
> A clothing for the soul divine;

and that 'Be thou strong and very courageous' is the best prescription for enduring joy.

The children's hymn that started rightly by stressing the wonder and beauty of life ends rightly by stressing challenge and growth as the only way to fuller joy:

> 'All that we need to do,
> Be we low or high,
> Is to see that we grow
> Nearer the sky.'

CHAPTER VII

EXPERIENCE OF TRUTH: ITS
RELATION TO SELF-KNOWLEDGE

Let us lay aside all arrogance. Let us not claim that we have
already discovered the Truth. Let us seek it as something which
is known to neither of us. For then only may we seek it lovingly
and tranquilly, if there be no bold presumption that it is already
discovered and possessed.

ST. AUGUSTINE.

'THIS CHILD, THE native of a Christian land, is worse
than many a little heathen who says its prayers to Brahma
and kneels before Juggernaut. This girl is—a liar.'

Poor little Jane Eyre! Her new school was quite alarming
enough without this public humiliation from the egregious
Mr. Brockenhurst. Moreover, the word 'liar' is, or was, a
very terrifying one to children, who knew from their Bibles
that the Devil is the father of lies and that 'all liars shall have
their part in the lake which burneth with fire and brim-
stone; which is the second death'.

This is the first, and often the last, association that many
children ever have with the word 'truth'—namely, the negative one that it is bad to tell lies. If, however, we examine the
word more carefully, we find there are several positive and
important things which we ought to realise about the
nature of truth.

In the first place, the truth is often exceedingly complex
and difficult to come by. 'Truth', said Abelard, 'has as many
coats as an onion.' It is also difficult to express. Therefore
when an angry adult says to a child, 'I want the exact truth,'

or when the law court asks for 'the truth, the whole truth and nothing but the truth', or when a religious group insists on 'absolute truth' regardless of consequences, all may be demanding the impossible. The child may not be able to find words; the witness may be uncertain and confused by the complexity of the situation; the Group member may rightly hesitate to overstep the bounds of discretion and of charity in making his 'absolute' confession. If the court witness tries his best to meet the demand for 'the whole truth', he is likely to earn the stern rebuke: 'Answer "Yes" or "No". Did you, or did you not?' He may try again with 'Yes. Only it wasn't quite like that. . . .' But the attempt to tell the full story as seen from every angle would take time, patience, and insight, and so the black-or-white, 'all-or-none' concept of truth, superficial and incomplete as it is, has to serve in the law courts for the most part. In thinking for ourselves about the nature of truth, we should try to go deeper.

In his biography of W. E. Ford, Beresford tells us that this great schoolmaster used to explain to his children that 'to tell a lie is the easy, unenterprising thing to do. The clever thing is to tell the truth so as to make oneself understood.' But to tell the truth about a complex situation requires more than cleverness; it requires a certain emotional attitude in the hearer as well as in the speaker: attitudes of humility, and a patient willingness to enter into the situation sympathetically.

A nice example of 'speaking the truth in love'—that is of expressing true facts in such a way as to make them acceptable—was once given by the wise Prince Consort when he stopped the true but inflammatory despatch from England to America during the Civil War. The Queen, looking only at the bald facts, protests: 'But, Albert, as we are in the right, what else can we do?' And Albert replies 'Alter a few words. . . . Say it; but say it differently. Often it's just the way a thing is said that decides whether it shall be peace or war.'

It cost Albert a night of strenuous effort and a mortal illness to find the successful way of 'saying it differently'.[1]

The truth cannot be spoken effectively about anything of importance unless speaker and hearer are on the same wavelength, have the same feeling for values, and want to understand each other. Where this condition does not exist, sometimes love and insight in the speaker can create it in the hearer, or vice versa. But when this is not possible, then words are futile and might better not be spoken. At his trial, Jesus wasted no words in His own defence, because He knew His judges were not interested in hearing what He had to say, and merely wanted Him out of the way as quickly as possible. The only person who would perhaps have liked to listen was Pilate. His enquiry as to the nature of truth was perhaps not mere cynicism. But had he waited for an answer, he might have become too sympathetically involved in the mind of the man he wanted to save, but dare not.

There are, too, so many different aspects of truth. The truth with which Jesus was concerned—the truth that He said would 'make us free'—was truth about meaning and values, an altogether different and deeper kind of thing than truth about matters of measurable fact, such as the speed of light or the price of cotton. These can be readily discovered by anyone with the necessary I.Q. But there is a form of truth which cannot be revealed by the analytic intellect alone: it must be sought with the total self. It cannot be told in answer to a question like Pilate's, for it is not an external thing or fact. It is emergent truth and will dawn on us with increasing clarity as we grow in understanding and insight.

The distinction is one of basic importance in education and in psychotherapy; it is the distinction between the instructor who believes that all we have to do is to tell the facts and the educator who believes there is a potential for creative growth within the human organism, a germ of selfhood, a capacity for ever-increasing awareness which can be stimulated into activity and the individual thereby be enabled to find truth for himself. The educator knows that unless the learner does seek for and with himself, then nothing of importance has taken place, no matter how much verbal information has been committed to memory.

The futility of the method of merely factual instruction receives constant illustration. A writer asks of a recent crime: 'Is it not a dreadful thing that these two brutal and callous murderers should both have had extremely religious upbringings?' Yes, indeed, it is a dreadful reflection; but it forces one to wonder sceptically about the type of religious 'education' to which they were exposed. 'Truth without charity is not of God', said Pascal. One is compelled to wonder how much charity there was in the upbringing of these murderers. Whatever true facts they may have been taught, such facts were obviously not converted into heart wisdom and loving-kindness. Sometimes religious knowledge is conducted in an atmosphere which contradicts its own central teaching that God is love. Often it consists primarily of mechanical memory exercises, isolated from all contact with relevant living experience.

Given the right kind of emotional receptivity, it is good to store the mind with fine literature. But the 'heart of education is the education of the heart', and if the material offered for memorising does not touch the deep springs of life, the feelings, then we get only learning by rote; the heart is not involved.

When language is inherently beautiful, like some of the Psalms, it will speak to the heart regardless of whether or not it is understood. If, however, it not only lacks beauty, but is factually boring, then it is educationally worthless. Thomas Mann, in *Buddenbrooks*, describes the sort of material regarded by 'educators' of his day as worthy of study—for example, that 'Job had seven thousand sheep, three thousand camels, five hundred yoke of oxen, five hundred she-asses, and a large number of servants'. Doubtless all true facts, but why wouldn't anyone become a criminal on such a diet?

Far, far better for children to be walking in the pastures among the oxen and the asses.

We must use words in the educative process, but if we use them without discrimination or discernment, without relation to the child's interests or experiences, then we are doing something worse than wasting time: we are boring children rather than illuminating them; dulling their minds so that they lose their power of fresh spontaneous reaction to life; and giving them the idea that learning is a dreary and tedious process that must be endured rather than enjoyed.

For a time, children will make very creditable attempts to introduce their own meaning into otherwise meaningless material. When required to give the story of Luke i. 7, in her own words, eight-year-old Susan wrote: 'Now, Elizabeth was a baroness, and because she was very strict, she had no children.' And such charming substitutions as 'Good Mrs. Murphy shall follow me all the days of my life' and 'Pontius the Pilot is driving this aeroplane' further illustrate the need to relate the words one hears to meaningful imagery and experiences.

We cannot, however, be purist in religious education and avoid all unexplained terms, for, even if that were desirable, life will not allow it. 'When I marry, I shall not have the word "God" mentioned in my house' was the decision of a college graduate who saw the impossibility of giving children 'truthful' answers, and the complications which must arise in consequence. But the name of God will inevitably creep into the most rational of homes, the following conversation shows how unnecessary it is to try and protect children from wrestling with unmanageable concepts. It was taken down verbatim by the house-mother of a nursery school for children from very rationalist homes. It is the expression of minds not yet 'fissured' into conscious and unconscious, and not troubled by considerations of logical consistency; imaginative minds to whom all life was an adventure to be explored.

Ann: God made the winds and the cold winds and He wears a kimona to keep Him warm.

Barbara: Yes; and God makes us laugh and cry and every-thing. He doesn't like it when we fall down.

A.: No, when we fall down, He gets a shake.

B.: God is inside everything you know: He is a tiny man.

A.: No: He's the whole world; and we're in the world, and He's the world and He's inside us.

B.: God is really our tummy.

Mary: No; God works on our food and makes it into blood. Barbara, wouldn't it be lovely if we were grown-up fairies and were married, and I was a father fairy, and you were a mother fairy and Jill was our baby fairy?

B.: Yes. I absolutely love God and Jesus, because God and Jesus and Mary everybody loves.

A.: Jesus is God, and Jesus was really a person.

B.: God hasn't got wings; He's got a little house in the sky and nobody knows how it keeps up; and it has little windows. Ann, do you know, God is the sun.

A.: I like you, Barbara, as much as everything. I like you as big as the world.

B.: Well, what do you think when you fight me?

A.: I'm never going to fight you again.

B.: All right. I'm going to sleep now.

A.: All right. We'll go on talking to-morrow.

In this delightful, spontaneous and inconsequential blend of theology, phantasy and moralising we see how freely the uninhibited infant mind uses imagery in the attempt to make meaning out of this astonishing and wonder-full world. There are at least five or six different word pictures of the Deity. He is 'a tiny man', 'the whole world', 'Jesus', 'inside us', 'the sun', 'our tummy'.

The identification of God with 'the whole world' and with 'the sun' savours of pantheism. This intuitive sense that God expresses Himself in the earth forces was also evident in three-year-old Bobbie, who enquired of his mother: 'Where does God live and what does He eat?' and immediately answered his own question with the information: 'He eats the trees and the sky.' Another infant, pointing to the round globe of the setting sun, asked 'That's God's head, isn't it, Mummy?' (Some two thousand years ago, the Greek philosopher Anaxagoras was ostracised for teaching that the sun was a red-hot stone and not a god.)

'Theology', therefore, appears to be inevitable. Even if we keep children clear of the theology of the Churches, we cannot protect them from the 'theology' of their own minds, where irrational images arise spontaneously in answer to need. That is why the attempt to abolish fairy stories on the ground that they are not 'true' is a losing battle. The unconscious will send along new images and stories as occasion requires, like the dear, comforting, imaginary yet 'real' old lady who lived in *The Mango Tree*[2] and all the imaginary companions who lived with children in *The Scarecrow*.[3] If anyone wonders why little children should love a man who lived two thousand years ago, there is the answer: the need of a Good Companion. Little Alan was suffering great pain after a severe operation. 'Does it hurt very much?' he was asked. 'Yes; it does; but I think of Jesus and that makes it better.'

We ought not, in the interest of truth, to try to 'purify' children's minds of all irrational images and concepts, or what we sweep out of the front door will reappear in new form at the back. What, then, should we do? Leave children with their 'nonsense' until they reach the age of reason? Yes, and no. Some images will fade naturally in time when the need for them does not any longer exist. But with others, what is required is an education which gradually deepens the child's intuitive understanding, so that he is enabled to deflect the emphasis from the image on to its significant meaning. For example, Terry, aged five, had learned somewhere that God was within her. 'Like my food?' she logically asked. 'No,' replied her wise mother. 'Like your heart.' That made sense, because Terry knew that the heart stood for love. Another mother whose little girl of six had been somewhat troubled by the Sunday school teacher's talk of God's ever-watchful eye, explained: 'Because people find it hard to think of something spiritual that they cannot touch or see, they talk about God as though He were a man, to make him more understandable to themselves. That is what people did in the old days when they first began to try and understand about God.' Later, after experiencing the pregnant quiet of a Friends' Meeting, this same child asked, 'What is God?' and her mother replied: 'Just as you are sure of my love and know it to be real, although you cannot see it, so I feel sure of the Spirit, God, behind all the Universe that we know.' And then, in order to show that the word used to express this Spirit is in itself unimportant, she added: 'Your father does not want to talk about that power of beauty and goodness by the name of God, but he believes in it and tries to live his life in faith with it.'⁴ (An additional step in freeing the child from any one word symbol or image would have been to tell her some of the 'thousand and one names' by which the Spirit has been known throughout the ages, so helping forward the realisation that what matters is not the word or the name, but the Reality behind it. In such ways 'theology' is kept flexible, tentative, non-authoritarian, continuously thoughtful, and more of a help than a hindrance in the search for truth.)

So much, then, for the distinction between truths of meaning and truths of fact. Both have their place, and one should not be regarded as superior to the other just because it can be verified by reason or by measurement. The concern of religion is with truths of meaning and of value. Meanings and values are also 'facts', though of a different order from the facts of science and history. When we conceive of religion as depending on a set of unchangeable statements, it ceases to be religion.

Another facet of truth to be considered is that of related-ness. This is a matter of greater concern to us to-day than ever before in history because the dangers of dissociation are greater. Specialisation, which has been defined as 'knowing more and more of less and less', has given us immense knowledge of the external world, but our knowledge and understanding of the inner world of man is relatively rudimentary. 'To-day we know the atom better than we know the mind that knows the atom',[5] with the result that our planet resembles a nursery school whose children have been given hand-grenades as playthings. Such has been our respect for the seeker in the realm of 'pure knowledge' that the research scientist has been accorded an almost reverent prestige. He has been encouraged to go ahead with his isolated pursuit regardless of whether we were ready for the consequences of his findings.

Love of truth for its own sake is a fine ideal if it includes all aspects of truth and the relations between them, but a great and dangerous gulf has come about between truths of the outer and of the inner worlds. When Sir Hiram Maxim was demonstrating his newly invented gun, a spectator asked him: 'But will not this make war very terrible?' 'No,' was the confident reply. 'It will make war impossible.' Sir Hiram's knowledge of human nature was badly out of line with his knowledge of firearms. Specialisation is inevitable and brings great value in its own sphere, but to achieve knowledge of the outer world without achieving an equal understanding of the inner is to create a perilous dislocation. In the fifth century, the Roman philosopher Boethius warned us that 'In other creatures ignorance of self is nature; in man it is a vice'. To-day the warning should be taken seriously, for the consequences of continuing to ignore it may be fatal. We now have so much more outer power to abuse, that it is no longer safe for us to remain in ignorance of the forces that motivate us, no longer permissible to try to escape self-knowledge by labelling introspection 'morbid'. 'Psycho-analysis', says Fromm, 'has given the concept of truth a new dimension.'[6] It has done so by demonstrating that only in proportion as we know the truth about ourselves can we really know the truth about anything or anyone else; that without a better understanding of ourselves, through personal exploration, we cannot know much about other people. Merely to have an intellectual knowledge of the mechanisms of the unconscious is not enough, for it is possible to have such knowledge without ever applying it to ourselves; to know about the unconscious mechanism of projection, but not to know when we are guilty of it. There is a sense in which truth, like beauty, is 'in the eye of the beholder', and if the eye itself is blurred and confused, then it cannot see anything clearly. What Fromm means is, not that everyone should be psychoanalysed, but that analysis has shown the necessity of becoming better aware of the unknown areas of the mind if we want to see truth more clearly; that conscious good intent is not enough because the unconscious, by a cunning process known as 'rationalisation', can blind us completely as to the nature of our real drives and motives. The fact that we are largely out of touch with the unconscious does not mean that it is out of touch with us. It influences and directs our conscious behaviour to an alarming extent; it dresses up our hidden hatreds and passions as lofty ideals and so convinces us that we really are what we like to imagine ourselves to be; and that other things and people are as we see them and as we wish them to be.

In this way the ideal of truth has been prostituted throughout history, and still to-day the Christian minister is not unknown who will use his 'religion' as a thin veil for his prejudices, and even to cover his political creed. An American radio preacher recently told his audience that Jesus would certainly be on the side of private enterprise 'because He believed in the individual'. There are others who label their own peculiar views 'Christian economics'.

'You will never lose faith', wrote Abbé Huvelin, 'if you always seek Truth, not your truth.' The reason this excellent advice is so difficult to follow is that, without knowing it, we prefer our own way and the realisation of our own desires to truth as such. It is generally felt that, if a man is sincere, then his words and deeds must have value. 'We know', says Bosanquet, 'the kind of man who, on the whole, gets nearest truth. It is not the cleverest; it is, I think, the sincerest.' The word 'sincere' has a good emotional 'aura' to it, but it is not enough to be sincere on the conscious level. Père Josef was sincere; so doubtless were Torquemada and Hitler and many other self-deluded paranoics. Of Dr. Hewlett Johnson, the 'Red Dean' of Canterbury, the Archbishop said in a speech which is a model of wise tolerance: 'He is sincere—passionately sincere—but he can no longer see himself, his views or political affairs objectively.' Another illustration of unconscious self-delusion in the sphere of religious thinking is given in the autobiography of Phyllis Bottome, where she writes: ' "Are you sure that God is as real to you as bread and butter?" I once asked my mother at an early age. She fixed her beautiful blue eyes on mine and told me that bread and butter were much less real to her than God. But even this failed to convince me, for if she believed in God, why was she so often afraid? For she was afraid. I knew this because I felt her fear in my own blood. I was part of her and I felt infected by her fear. Yet I knew, long before the text was impressed on me from without, that love and fear are incompatible. . . . My father and mother both taught me a great deal about their religion, but what I actually learnt was that my mother was afraid of life and my father was highly irresponsible. . . . Hymns, texts, collects and Catechism rolled from our lips with almost uncanny ease. In spite of these . . . the acid test of religion was not met by these two unequivocally religious people.'[7]

This passage reminds us again that words are not the most potent means of education; that what we are speaks more loudly than what we say. The mother was not consciously hypocritical; she was simply unaware of the gap, sensed by her child, that existed between her protestations and her realisation of them in life—a gap that exists in all of us. With her uncle, the child's relationship was more solid, because he made fewer pretensions. ' "Uncle George, what makes you believe Christianity is true?" Silent for a long time, his eyes at last met mine with the directness of an equal. "I think there is some evidence in Church history for the truth of Christianity, and perhaps even more in each person's individual conscience. This you must find out for yourself.'' '8

Such frank objectivity about religious truth is rare, but is more likely to engender a similar objectivity in the child than would any dogmatic statement. There would be no danger of religious belief collapsing like a pack of cards in later life if children were not asked to subscribe to more than their inner experience and personal research seemed to justify at each stage of development. We shall get nearer to truth when all aspects of knowledge are studied in their relationship to each other, and most of all when knowledge of ourselves is no longer ignored, but is considered a serious area for research and one which desperately needs to catch up with our knowledge of the external world.

While we must ever be seeking for further truth, we must at the same time be content with partial truth. 'To grasp at ultimate truth is to be for ever empty-handed.'9 Therefore, like Father Tyrrell, we have to learn to be 'content to be much in the dark', for, as St. Paul said long ago, 'At present all we see is the baffling reflection of reality; we are like men looking at a landscape in a small mirror. The time will come when we shall see reality whole and face to face. At present all I know is a little fraction of the truth, but the time will come when I shall know it as fully as God now knows me.'10

The Church has been at fault whenever it has given us the impression that it has all the answers, and that more knowledge is available to us about ultimate realities than is in fact the case or than we have earned the right to at our elementary stage of development. 'Our knowledge is a torch of smoky pine',11 and we must be content to have it so and not complain that the soul receives nothing but a 'dusty answer':

'When hot for certainties in this our life.'12

For we are not entitled to any answers that we do not, like Parsifal, go out and win for ourselves by our own search; and these answers, so far as the meaning of life and the nature of ultimate reality is concerned, will be proximate rather than final because our knowledge and experience must inevitably stop with the limitations of our humanity. Therefore we should 'eschew the unattainable' while at the same time we continually work at enlarging our capacity for apprehension. We can absorb of truth, as of beauty, only so much as we are ready for. A Manchester tripper once accosted a university professor who was revelling in the beauties of the Lake District with the angry question: 'Is there anything to see in this place?' A truthful if unkind answer would have been: 'For you, as you are at present, no, there is nothing to see. You will have first to take a "voyage to the interior" and to do a considerable amount of work on yourself before you see what I do, which also is only a small portion of all that there is to see.'

No truth then can be ours until we have experienced it, until it enters into our lives and becomes a part of us. Therefore we cannot force the pace or take impatient short-cuts for if we do our fate will be the same as that of the poor dragonfly for whom a kindly but too hasty observer cut open the chrysalid case before it had acquired strength enough to fly.

Havelock Ellis rather grimly compares our journey towards truth to that of a cheese-mite working its way through cheese. 'Even a cheese-mite, one imagines, could only with difficulty obtain an adequate conception of a cheese (yet it goes on working its way through). How much more difficult the task is for man whose everyday intelligence seems to move on a plane so much like that of a cheese-mite and yet has so vastly more complex a web of phenomena to synthesize.'[13]

The prospect looks at times so depressing that the poet writes a melancholy description of 'The Seekers':

'Not for us are content, and quiet, and peace of mind,
For we go seeking a city that we shall never find.

'There is no solace on earth for us, for such as we
Who search for a hidden city that we shall never see.'[14]

The picture is a half-truth, for though we shall not see the
City of God with clarity in this life (why should we expect
to?), we can glimpse its spires afar as they occasionally
'flash through the encircling gloom', and this gives enough
light 'to guide our steps into the way of truth'. 'Seek and ye
shall find' was no empty promise, for the search is never
wasted, even when we seem to be finding nothing. In education, it is of the utmost importance to give children this
concept of truth-finding as a lifelong adventure, a joyous
exploration, to let them experience for themselves the thrill
of discovery in every sphere. 'Oh, I see now,' suddenly
exclaimed seven-year-old Ursula in the midst of a Scripture
lesson. 'God didn't really want Abraham to offer up his
son; Abraham only *thought* he did.' Her flash of insight had
produced a 'pearl' of wisdom which she shared as joyously
with the class as the woman in the parable shared the discovery of her lost coin. Strange to say, this seven-year-old's
discovery was one that many adults never make—namely,
that our concept of God varies with our stage of development
and is contingent on our level of thought and feeling; that,
as Rilke expressed it, 'Thou growest with my maturity'.
Another child's attempt to make the story morally acceptable was to reverse the position and make God do the
growing up: 'I suppose that was before God became a
Christian?' she asked.

The child to whom the religious life is presented as a way,
a search, is infinitely less vulnerable to traumatic loss of faith
than one to whom religion is presented as a fixed and static
creed embodying final truth and to be believed unquestion-
ingly. The acceptance of the religious life as a continuous
search which each individual must undertake for himself
seems to be more natural to the Eastern way of thought than
to the West.

This emergent view of the God of Truth will not appeal

to minds that can be happy only with the tidy and definite medieval cosmology to which they have become accustomed; minds to which the mysteries of the Kingdom are no mysteries, but concrete, clear-cut, categorical matters of fact, with no loose ends and no unanswered questions. It is, however, more in accordance with the teaching of Jesus on the nature of the Kingdom as something invisible, inward and spiritual. The germ of this teaching on the seed of the Kingdom can be planted in all minds, especially in the minds of the young and receptive. Whether it will grow depends, as the parable of the Sower tells us, on the nature of the soil. If there is no 'depth of earth' it cannot take root.

CHAPTER VIII

EXPERIENCE OF GOODNESS: I. ITS DEPENDENCE ON INTEGRATION OF THE PERSONALITY

He who is not himself a unity is never really anything wholly and decisively.

KIERKEGAARD.

THE STUDY OF THE ultimate nature of the good is the sphere of ethics and of religion. Religion, in the words of the prophet Micah, gives us a clear-cut statement: 'He hath shown thee and man what is good . . . to love justice, to do mercy, and to walk humbly.' And although we are far from knowing what is just, and are often in grave doubt as to when and how much we ought to show mercy, we do on the whole subscribe to these first two values. About humility we are no longer so sure.

Our concern in this chapter is not with the nature of the good as such, but with our failure to achieve it or to implement the values and ideals to which we do lip service.

Like humility, goodness has 'lost her looks of late'. Among the 'intellectuals', being an interesting person has of recent years been valued more highly than being a good one. A young mother, collecting her small son after his first day at a nursery school, asked anxiously, 'Has he been a good boy?' The teacher murmured a rebuke and hastily changed the conversation. Later she explained: 'We do not ask that question nowadays; we ask: Is he happy and well-adjusted?' For if he was, then, she implied, there could be no problem

131

of anti-social behaviour. 'Goodness' was an out-of-date concept no longer employed by the enlightened. This same attitude was expressed by a bright young woman at a cocktail party. 'Good?' she smiled. 'The word has no meaning. Its one of those value-judgement words. They're out. They're as Victorian as . . . let's say as psychology before Freud! What can you mean?'[1]

Why has goodness gone under this cloud of disapproval? Why does the heroine in a modern novel embarrass us with the announcement: 'I refuse to be ashamed of goodness any longer?' Why are articles written on 'The Harm that Good Men do?' Perhaps the answer is in part due to a realisation that a great deal of hypocrisy has come to be connected with the term; that a façade of superficially 'good' behaviour can be used to cover up very unpleasant qualities. The brief neighbourly dialogue: 'She's a *good* woman.' 'Yes. I don't like her either'—showed an unadmitted awareness of this device, as did the child's prayer: 'O God, please make the bad people good, and make the good people nice.'

The lens of analytic psychology has laid bare the mind's unconscious trick of disguising its less-civilised motives even from itself and of dressing them up in the garments of virtuous phraseology so that they cannot very easily be challenged.

Then, again, it is clear that adults have often tied the label 'good' to those forms of behaviour which suited their own convenience. A 'good' child was one who accepted those labels without question, and meekly did what he was told. On a school report 'Conduct good' simply meant: 'Has kept all the rules and given no trouble.' The samplers of an earlier age made the matter quite explicit:

> 'Let children that would fear the Lord
> Hear what their teachers say;
> With reverence meet their parents' word
> And with delight obey.

132

'For those who worship God, and give
　　Their parents honour due,
　Here on this earth they long shall live,
　　And live hereafter too.'

The Catechism was equally explicit: 'My duty is . . . to
submit myself to all my governors, teachers, spiritual
pastors and masters: To order myself lowly and reverently
to all my betters.'

Let us frankly admit that the facet of goodness known as
obedience is a necessary expedient in any form of social life.
Without a certain amount of it, no family could survive.
Adult nervous systems can only stand so much youthful
ebullience, and children do not in fact always know what is
best for them. But when obedience is made the one and all-
important virtue, when it is so stressed that it inhibits the
functioning of intelligence, as in the sad story of Casabianca,
then it has certainly been over-valued in relation to other
virtues.

But exploration into the hidden ways of the psyche
reveals an astonishing gulf between outward behaviour and
inner feeling, and we can no longer be at all sure that the
obedient child is 'good'. Apparent amenability and sweet-
ness may be nothing but a façade behind which dwell fears,
anxieties and resentments which, if not brought into consciousness, accepted and dealt with, will live on and some
day surprise everybody by breaking through and demanding
expression. The unconscious is never mocked, and will, in
its own way and time, take heavy toll for the treatment it
has received, for the failure of the conscious self to recognise
and come to a workable arrangement with it. The dark
continents of our minds cannot be permanently kept hidden
and ignored. If not integrated with the total person, they
will one day break loose and smash the charming façade
with which we face the world. An alarming illustration of
this is the recent case of the sixteen-year-old American
baby-sitter who strangled the sleeping child in her charge.

When asked, 'Why did you do it?' she gave the bewildered reply: 'I don't know. I had to. I'm sorry now.' One part of herself had committed a terrible crime without the knowledge or approval of her conscious self. 'She was', said the report, 'overcome by an irresistible impulse'; an impulse unguessed at by herself and by her friends and relatives. In fact, so effective was her *persona* that her doctor described her as 'well-groomed, mild and modest'. No one doubted that she was 'good' enough to be given responsibility. In another recent case no one doubted the reliability of the head boy of the remand home who later became a murderer.

Such extreme cases of dissociation are fortunately rare in peacetime society, but in less violent forms they are not so rare as we would like to think. Wherever a part of the self is split off as it were from the main stream of consciousness in order to create a façade or pseudo-self which will placate society, the individual becomes to some extent confused, and loses touch with his original self. He functions now from two different 'selves' or centres: his real self which wants to grow and become, and which is the source of all effort, interest, and creativity, fights for its life and fights in the dark, against the self which threatens to destroy it. In extreme cases, as we have seen, the severance is complete; the individual no longer knows who he is, what his real feelings are, what he truly wants, or why he behaves as he does. 'He did not know what he was doing or why', reported the authorities on the child-killer who recently escaped from Broadmoor, and repeated his crime. Less extreme cases of neurosis, psychosis, drug addiction, delinquency, etc., are all expressions of the same failure to become aware of, to integrate, control and sublimate powerful instinctual needs or drives.

Dissociation is a widespread condition, and even among 'normal' people Freud says, the whole of society is suffering from it to some degree. He tells us what a profound shock it was to civilised men everywhere to watch the lights of Europe go out once again in 1914. It was generally assumed that twentieth-century man had outgrown his murderous impulses and was capable of a rational discussion and negotiation of his problems, but to our dismay this assumption was shown to be ill-founded.

We should not have been so surprised had we realised the true facts. Writing in 1916, Freud gave this startling diagnosis: 'In reality, our fellow citizens have not sunk so low as we feared, because they had never risen so high as we believed. . . . Man is living psychologically beyond his means because the pace has been forced too high. Therefore when he falls he appears to fall very low; whereas really he is only returning to the earlier conditions of emotional life and functioning where uneducated passions hold sway.'[2] In other words, war is mankind's accepted convention for the release of those passions that have never been accepted and educated and which therefore remain in their primeval form just below the threshold of consciousness.

Obviously the mass of people taking part in war are not dangerous repressed savages at the mercy of their passions: they are rather at the mercy of those who start and drive the war machine. But at the same time it is true that 'We are misled by our optimism into grossly exaggerating the number of human beings who have been transformed in a civilised sense'—that we do in fact all have more 'shadow' in our make-up than we are normally aware of. On this point both Jung and Freud are agreed. Jung tells us: 'If modern man turns his gaze inward upon the recesses of his own mind, he will discover a chaos and a darkness there which he would gladly ignore. . . . To accept himself in all his wretchedness is the hardest of tasks.'[3] And Freud affirms: 'The truth is that men are not gentle, friendly creatures . . . who simply defend themselves if attacked, but that a powerful desire for aggression has to be reckoned with as part of their instinctual endowment. . . . *Homo homini lupus.* . . . Civilised society is perpetually menaced by this primary hostility of men towards one another.'[4] These statements must sound very extreme to the ordinary decent and respectable citizen, but Goethe is reported to have said that there was no crime of which he did not feel himself capable.

How does this dissociation come about in our being? When and where does it start? When and how do young children lose the wholeness which was theirs at the beginning? There is, of course, more than one cause. Sometimes it may be a case of suffering that could not be met, grief that could not be assimilated or understood. A child whose parents were planning separation, sat listlessly before his fragmented drawing of a horse. When asked why tail, legs and body were all disconnected, he at first replied, 'I don't know why,' and then, after a pause, added, 'Nothing I love is together.' Another boy, also the victim of a broken home, expressed his deep, inmost anxiety by drawing a sinking ship with the sails torn down and the mast broken. A girl of seven with the same shattering experience behind her was well on the way to becoming a 'problem child' at school, where she gave vent to her misery by causing trouble to others. At home she took refuge in phantasy and wrote fairy stories in which the father, after wandering alone in a dark wood, at last found his lost wife and joyfully carried her safely home to peace and security. In her unconscious, she reverted to infantile modes of behaviour (thumb-sucking, etc.) in order to recover the happiness and wholeness of infancy. Her sufferings remained largely dissociated from her conscious self until adolescence, when, with the help of sympathetic understanding, she was able to talk about them.

All these cases indicate that the child feels his home to be a unitary organism, held together by an unalterable love. If that love ceases and his home breaks up, the foundations of his world give way and religious life is damaged accordingly. For it is in the home that the sense of unity with others first develops, and the experience of a breakdown there can be as alarming, and considerably more bitter, than loss by death itself. 'I trust nobody now,' remarked one small boy whose faith in parental loyalty had been shattered. Even if the break in parental affection does not reach the law courts, it can still destroy any stable basis for happiness, as with the four-year-old boy who spent the morning at his nursery school painting black smears because his parents had quarrelled again at breakfast. (The arts, whether painting, modelling, movement, drama, or writing, are proving more and more valuable in revealing to the trained eye the presence and the nature of emotional trouble in children, as in mental patients. This does not mean that expression automatically results in the disappearance of the trouble, but it does bring it in the open and thereby enable the skilled adult to help the child deal with it and to try to integrate rather than to repress it.)

Another fertile cause of the dissociated or 'split' mind lies in the fact that the child cannot keep pace with adult demands. The standards demanded are forced too high too soon. What is responsible for this unreasonable and harmful pressure? In some parents it is over-anxiety, in others a craving to domineer. Both are bent on having a 'good' child, which often means simply one that will be approved of by self and neighbours. And so with a mistaken psychology that regards the mind of the new-born infant as a wax tablet or a clean sheet of paper, the parent announces confidently: 'It's all a matter of forming correct habit patterns.' The blatantly power-loving parent adds: 'The first thing to do is to let the child know I'm master.'

One might have supposed that with the excessive shock of arrival in a new world, 'the trauma of birth', and the task of learning to adapt to this strange new environment outside the immediate protection of the mother's body, the newly born infant would have enough in the way of difficulty to keep him 'disciplined' for the time being. Yet so strong is the urge in some adults to train up a child in the way they want him to go, and to prevent the poor babe from thinking that he can 'get by' with anything, that they can hardly wait to start the moulding process on what they wrongly conceive as the passive clay of the child's mind. 'I never give her anything until she smiles for it,' boasted one father of his infant daughter, as if he were training a dog to beg. Thus, even in the cradle, the dividing process may begin: the process of hiding from one's parents or their substitutes those modes of behaviour which will meet with disapproval. The one thing the child cannot afford to lose at this tender age is love and approval. According to his temperament and the strength of his relative needs, he pretends to take on standards which his instinctive nature is very far from accepting.

At the same time, he begins to 'hate' those who so deprive him of his instinctual satisfactions. Thus he develops those ambivalent feelings which become a further source of trouble, in that this 'hatred' must also be hidden both from its recipients and from himself. He begins to acquire a capacity to play two roles: one which will satisfy authority, and one to his own satisfactions in furtive concealment.

The hypocrisy engendered in this way is not necessarily altogether unconscious. It depends on the stage of growth, the strength of the ego, and the intensity of the feelings involved. A conscious hypocrite is not an attractive indi- vidual, but he is probably in less danger of breakdown and less of a menace to society than the one who does not even know that he has undesirable anti-social drives dwelling behind his *persona* and biding their time for recognition and satisfaction. The odious little boy in *Jane Eyre* when asked, 'Would you rather have a verse of the Psalms to learn or a gingerbread nut to eat?' sanctimoniously replied, 'Oh the verse of a Psalm! Angels sing psalms. I wish to be a little angel here below.' His assumed piety appears to have taken in his unperceptive father, but it is doubtful if the child was as yet deluding himself. The probability is that he would grow up into a person with no real appreciation of values, but with a very clear idea of what paid and of how to keep an eye always open to the main chance.

In contrast, the young man who, when invited to consider his own faults instead of dwelling exclusively on those of others, blandly and with conscious 'sincerity' replied, 'I haven't any,' was in much greater danger both to himself and to society because of the complete separation which had come about between his conscious *persona* and his unconscious drives.

The long, slow and difficult process of reintroducing the separated parts of the personality to each other and of rendering them acceptable to each other, so that the individual may once again be whole instead of divided, is undertaken in the therapy of psychoanalysis. How therapeutic this process may prove to be depends largely on the strength of the love of the good in the patient in question. Love of the good may be innately weak, or it may have been too seriously damaged for full recovery. In the latter case the individual may be integrated, but not healed. The whole (or holy) life does not make a strong enough appeal to animate all life's forces on the side of the good. While stressing the fact that integration is essential to integrity, that only a person in contact with his entire nature can function wholesomely, it must also be noted that integration and integrity are not identical. It is possible to be well aware of our less reputable motivations and to be quite undisturbed by them. Frederick 'the Great', for example, did not even bother to be a hypocrite. When asked for an explanation of his outrageous conduct in invading the neighbouring state of Silesia, he replied cheerfully, 'Oh, ambition, and the desire to hear myself talked about.' In his case, we may perhaps explain while we do not excuse, this identification, with his own 'lower nature' as a natural result of the brutal treatment he received in youth from his father. But we cannot explain or excuse such activity as a result of a divided personality, for he knew what he did and why. He was integrated with his instinctive drives and at peace with them. This integration at the lowest level was the 'solution' of Lucifer: 'Evil, be thou my good.' It is a more serious 'solution' than a state of division within the self, for while there is division and conflict there is a chance of struggle and growth. Alcibiades is another famous example of a brilliant young man failing to live up to his own best standards. He seems, however, to have suffered a little more conflict about it than did Frederick, for he admitted that whenever he was with Socrates his soul was so stirred that he was angry with himself and his slavish state. 'This Marsyas has often brought me to such a pass that I have felt as if I could hardly endure the life which I am leading. . . . But when I leave his presence, the love of popularity gets the better of me.'[5]

A breakdown resulting from such a state of conflict can sometimes be a blessing in disguise, in that it forces the individual to face up to himself, to try to find out who he is and what he really wants to do with his life. For such a one there is always hope, in that, whatever his age, he can begin the integrative process, and achieve, if he has the will to persevere, at least that measure of wholeness of which his nature is capable.

For in all men there is, as well as the backward, the forward pull; as well as resentment and hate, there is the need to love and be loved; as well as inertia, there is the desire to go forward, to learn and to become; as well as jealousy and ambition, there is the desire to participate and cooperate with others. In fact, modern scientific comment assures us that 'our drives towards goodness are as biologically determined as our drives towards breathing',[6] just as inherent in our protoplasm, and certainly just as essential to our well-being and the well-being of society.

Goodness, therefore, is quite respectable after all; we need not be ashamed of it, but we do need to get a clearer idea both of what it is and of what blocks its expression. Most of all we need to reconsider the wisdom of the ages that has always insisted that goodness is a matter of hard work. The 'Brave New Worlders', who believe that everybody will be good if given economic equality, or if given more freedom, or if sensibly handled in youth, or if well fed and clothed are seeing but a half-truth. All these things are important in their degree, but we do not make people good merely by making them comfortable. Certainly there are external conditions of misery which make goodness supremely difficult, if not impossible. But to change such conditions, although essential, will not solve the total problem, for the simple reason that human nature is not simple and cannot be mechanically 'conditioned'. The instinctive urges of greed, aggression, jealousy and hate emphasised by Freud and Jung are still operative, even in the most egalitarian and best administered of communities. They do not readily surrender to those contrary urges of loving and sharing merely by changing the external conditions.

Stevenson's 'Good Boy' whose simple trying would be regarded by the sophisticated as touchingly naïve, was in fact less naïve than his critics. For Stevenson knew what wise men have told us down the ages, but what some modern theorists have tried to side-step—namely, that

'In the field of this body, a great war is toward
Against anger, passion, pride, and greed,'[7]

or that, as the Greek poet Hesiod wrote some 800 years B.C., 'Vice may be had in abundance without trouble, for the way is smooth and her dwelling-place is near; but before virtue the gods have set toil'. This is not a welcome truth, and so to avoid its implications we continue to invent superficial theories about human nature and how it may be changed from the outside.

Nevertheless, the toil and conflict and struggle in trying to achieve goodness could be considerably less arduous and less traumatic if, in addition to improving the external conditions of society, as we must, we also achieved a clearer idea of the dynamics of emotional life and of what is involved in a process of disciplined and wholesome growth. The following example illustrates the kind of wise and loving handling which can enable even a very young child to accept and work on her emotions without having to hide them from her parents or herself: A young mother went into the nursery, to find her little daughter vigorously pounding a baby brother. Realising the intensity of the child's jealousy, the mother was able to refrain from violence in her own reaction. When things were quiet, she took the girl on her knee and said, 'I know how you feel; new babies are a nuisance and seem to take your mother from you. Most older children feel this way. It's not bad to have these feelings; it's only bad if you let them have you, if you give in to them. Try hitting a cushion next time, because the cushion won't mind. We all have to work on our feelings and not let them run away with us, like wild horses that have broken loose.'

Thus, by accepting the jealousy and resentment, the mother prevented them from being repressed into a separate compartment of the mind and their existence denied by the child's conscious ego. Instead, she presented the training of the emotions as an interesting process which had to be undertaken by everybody. Had she shown a shocked disapproval, the child would have felt further rejected and perhaps threatened with a permanent loss of love. To avoid the latter, she might have resorted to the subterfuge of pretending to behave in a way that would have secured her mother's approval, but without any real change in the quality of her emotion. The rebellion and jealousy could still remain guilty and undissipated beneath the surface. As it was, she felt loved and understood, but at the same time challenged to do some work on herself and not to allow the natural aggressiveness to triumph.

Not to give children standards to try to live up to is just as foolish and just as unfair as to expect too much from them. In their anxiety to prevent repressions and dissociations, some parents fall over backwards in not only refusing ever to prohibit or rebuke, but even in refusing to give direction or suggestion. In view of this new-fashioned danger, let it here be repeated that young children can become very bewildered from lack of wise guidance, and that they will sometimes go to extremes of 'bad behaviour' in order to force the too liberal parent to take a stand and give some clear guidance as to what is permissible and what is not. A class of boys in an American school recently made life so intolerable for their over-permissive teacher that he was obliged to resign. They then presented him with a handsome parting gift, and to the puzzled authorities vouchsafed this explanation: 'He was a swell guy. We liked him a lot. But he couldn't keep order, and we like somebody who can keep us in order.'

A similar case was that of a fourteen-year-old boy who turned angrily on his mother for giving him permission to go and see Aristophanes' *Lysistrata* if he wanted. 'I knew it,' he complained. 'There is nothing you won't let me do. Why can't you have some standards like other boys' mothers?'

On the other hand, parents can do serious damage to their children by presenting standards too lofty and too difficult of achievement. Such standards are often the projection of the adults' own unconscious, unrealised hopes and ambitions. To force the pace of virtue in order to show the world 'my perfect child', the thing I myself never became, but will now become through this extension of myself into my offspring, is to court disaster. A sorrowful elderly couple whose lives had been shattered by the suicide of their twenty-year-old son, constantly repeated to themselves the comforting but delusionary words: 'He was too good; that was all that was the matter with him.' They proudly told of their perfectionist standards for him, but they could not face the fact that he had been unable to meet those standards and dare not tell them so. Therefore they continued to console themselves with the same old phantasy of the 'perfect son'. They were quite convinced that they had truly loved their child, but such love is neither pure nor true, and is too often blended with a strong admixture of unrecognised and unacknowledged needs and hungers in the would-be perfect lover. Children cannot grow freely where parents, while loving, are also using them as a projection of their own unconscious needs.

Whatever the true and complete nature of goodness, and whatever else it is dependent on, it cannot exist save where there is integration of the personality as a whole. There cannot be spiritual health without mental health, and mental health in turn depends upon self-knowledge, on not allowing one part of ourselves to function in isolation from another part.

CHAPTER IX

EXPERIENCE OF GOODNESS:
II. ITS RELATION TO A LARGER INTEGRATION WITH THE 'NOT-SELF'

The emotions of the soul can leave man shut up within himself absorbed in his own feelings and beliefs, which are distinct from divine realities. Only spiritual experience can liberate the human soul and transform his subjective feelings into real ontological contacts with the spiritual world.

NICOLAS BERDYAEV: *Freedom and the Spirit*, p. 77.

WE HAVE SEEN THAT goodness is proportionate to the degree of wholeness that we can achieve through self-knowledge, and that education should therefore try to avoid making unnecessary fissures in the child's field of consciousness. But this is not at all to say that life will then become smooth and free from conflict. For however much we succeed in removing conflict and maladjustment in the early stages of existence, the process of adaptation cannot in the nature of things be continuously smooth, and we should not try to make it so. Very soon, infantile drives will have to start giving way to the demands of society. They will not do so willingly. Conflict and suffering are therefore inevitable and are the lot of everybody in some degree. Even if we could create the perfect world, perfection of adjustment to it would, we are told, be death to further evolution.

In the field of biology, for example, Le Comte de Nouy tells us: 'It is not the being best adapted to his environment who contributes to evolution. He survives, but his better adaptation eliminates him from the ascendant progression, and only contributes to increase the number of more or less stagnant species that people the earth. That smoothness of adaptation may be a hindrance to further advance is illustrated by the pre-Cambrian sandworms, who achieved a very successful adaptation to their environment, and then, having no reason to transform themselves further, they subsisted almost without a change for hundreds of millions of years. One of these worms, however, continued to evolve because it was less well adapted than the others, and probably possessed a kind of instability which did not constitute an advantage at the time, but which was conducive to still greater changes, and could be called "creative instability". This worm, less perfect as a worm, may have been our ancestor.'[1]

There are modern psychologists whose findings would appear to support those of de Nouy. Kretschmer, for example in his study of *Men of Genius*, produces abundant evidence to illustrate the thesis that the highly creative mind is one suffering from extreme tensions; and Dr. W. H. Rivers writes: 'We have, I think, reason to believe that the person who has attained perfection of balance in the control of his instinctive tendencies, in whom the processes of suppression and sublimation have become wholly effective, may thereby become completely adapted to his environment, and attain a highly peaceful and stable existence. Such existence is not, however, the condition of exceptional accomplishment, for which there would seem to be necessary a certain degree of instability of the unconscious and subconscious strata of the mind which form the scene of the conflict between instinctive tendencies and the forces by which they are controlled. . . . I believe we may look to this instability as the source of energy from which we may expect great accomplishments in art and science.'[2] This seems closely in line with de Nouy's statement that instability is essential to civilisation, that perfect adaptation would spell the end of progress.

The matter needs fuller investigation, for it would seem that some creative artists, such as Bach, have been both stable and happy. What we can say without question is that difficulty is an inescapable ingredient in the life of civilised man, and that learning how to carry conflict and to avoid rushing into premature solutions of our problems is the mark of a mature mind. (This is the theme of Dr. W. H. Sheldon's study, *Psychology and the Promethean Will*.) It is interesting to note that Freud is reported to have found ease boring and difficulty a necessary stimulus in his work: 'A failure (in research work) makes one inventive, creates a free flow of associations.'[3]

That all sounds very fine and encouraging as one reads it in a book, but living it is a different matter. We can admit the danger of rushing into premature and superficial 'solutions' in order to escape the tension of indecision. We can also see that, though we wish it were otherwise, pain and effort are somehow intertwined with character and creative advance—that a person who knows nothing of suffering is inadequate as a person. But must we not also admit that there is a limit to human endurance and that sometimes people are asked to go beyond that limit? In recent wars, for example, children have been subjected to hideous cruelties from which the normal mind turns in horror, unable to dwell on them or to fit them into any religious philosophy of life.

There is no answer to unendurable suffering. We must admit frankly that, at our present stage of existence and level of understanding, it is unendurable and we do not always know what to do about it. We cannot deal with these most appalling things in life directly, only indirectly by changing ourselves, at the same time doing what we can to improve the lot of others. We are told that Jesus wept over Jerusalem, foreseeing what was coming to it. He found he could not change the hearts and minds of men; and we are no nearer to knowing how to do it than He. So we flounder on from one war to the next in a morass of unchastened emotions of distrust, greed and fear. It would indeed seem true that 'we have no power of ourselves to help ourselves' and so look around desperately for some outside saviour who has 'the answer'. We turn from Karl Marx to Karl Barth, from the Kremlin to the Pope; but always in the end we find we must do the work of cleaning these Augean stables for ourselves. But not by ourselves. There is help available, and we should not let the inscrutable suffering of life blind us to what can be done to transcend suffering on the spiritual as well as on the material plane. It has been said that most men to-day go about in a mood of 'quiet desperation'. That is understandable, but not very helpful. They may feel they are being realistic, but what if there are realities that they are ignoring because their eyes are looking to the ground, and because they 'know' that to look anywhere else is wishful thinking and escapism?

There is an old match trick in which six matches are placed on a table and one is required to make them into four triangles. This is an impossibility save by changing one's approach and using a new dimension, thus forming a pyramid: 'the way out is the way up'.

The same is true of life. Its insoluble problems will remain insoluble so long as we stick to the horizontal plane. There is no answer on that level. But if we can rise a little higher, take, as it were, another hairpin bend up the mountainside and thus enlarge our range of vision, the facts may begin to emerge differently, and with every further ascent—that is, with every enlargement of consciousness— this becomes truer. The terrible things on the plain below are still there; the facts have not changed, but we change as we raise and expand our level of consciousness and so see the facts in a larger framework. This is what Pompilia meant when she cried in her wretchedness:

'Leave help to God, as I am forced to do,
There is no other help, or we should craze,
Seeing such evil with no human cure.'

Not, of course, to an omnipotent Person who could help matters if He would, but to that invisible, incomprehensible Power in which we feel ourselves to live and move and have our being.

Jesus' parable of the miraculous draught of fishes carries the same teaching. The Disciples had toiled all night in the same locality to no avail. They had given up hope, but in the morning they were told to try another approach, to launch out into the deep and cast their nets 'on the other side of the ship'. Whatever the spatial metaphor employed, the meaning is the same: try again, but in a different way. There are depths—or heights—of experience from which a problem can be not so much solved as outgrown, transcended, because it is seen in a new perspective, and in relation to new vision.

Perhaps the toiling through the night was a necessary preparation for this enlargement of vision. It was Goethe who said:

'Who never ate his bread with sorrow,
Who never spent the midnight hours
Watching and waiting for the morrow,
He knows you not, ye heavenly powers.'

What is certain is that merely to toil and endure on the plane of the here and now is not enough to make tolerable our deepest griefs or to solve our fiercest problems, and it is not surprising that many feel that if that is all life has to offer, then life is not acceptable on such terms.

It is not all life has to offer. There is a better answer than either suicide or stark endurance if we can achieve the desire, not merely to accept life, but to co-operate actively with it. This involves faith, however faint, that it is worth while to let down the net still once more, to venture on unknown seas, or, to change the metaphor, it involves a willingness to listen 'with the third ear'. The poet may be right that—

'The drift of pinions, would we harken,
Beats at our own clay-shuttered doors'[4]

and the saint that 'The breeze of God's grace is always
blowing. The active and the strong always keep the sails of
their minds unfurled to catch the favourable wind.'[5]

Each one who glimpses this truth can select the imagery
that appeals to him as most telling, and then meditate on it
and let its meaning unfold. To the Chinese, the secret of the
powers of growth latent in the psyche, powers which would
transcend evil and pain, was symbolised as a golden flower.
'The Secret of the Golden Flower', or the soul, is its power
to make light circulate; to unfold and receive light from the
Centre or Source, and then to change it into the new Light
of spiritual consciousness.

Whatever the metaphor, this is the meaning of that
larger integration with God or good or, for those who prefer
noncommital terms, with the 'not-self', which is necessary to
wholeness in triumph over pain. This is the 'over-belief'
on which William James said that he was willing to make his
personal venture—the belief, namely, that 'our present
consciousness is only one out of many worlds of consciousness
that exist, and that those other worlds must contain experiences that have a meaning for our life also; and that,
although in the main these experiences and those of this
world keep discrete, yet the two become continuous at
certain points, and higher energies filter in'. And then he
adds the pragmatic test: 'By being faithful in my poor
measure to this over-belief, I seem to keep myself more sane
and true.'

This is the language of the scientist describing not merely
what he thinks there is good ground for believing, but what
the effect of such belief is on his living. To-day Jung, in the
same tradition, stresses the necessity of avoiding religious
terminology in describing this experience of something
beyond, because it reminds his patients too much of what
they have to reject. 'I must', he says, 'express myself in

more modest terms, and say that the psyche has awakened to spontaneous life. . . . To the patient it is nothing less than a revelation when, from the hidden depths of the psyche, something arises to confront him—something strange that is not the "I" and is therefore beyond the reach of personal caprice. He has gained access to the sources of psychic life . . . a light shines through the confusion; from this point forward, the sufferer can reconcile himself with the warfare within and so come to bridge the morbid split in his nature on a higher level',⁶ or, we might also add, come to endure 'intolerable' suffering through a power greater than his own.

It is on this very fundamental fact of the life of the spirit that Jung parts company from Freud, who, he says, 'Shipwrecks on the question of Nicodemus'. Freud does not raise the question of the meaning of life and find its answer in terms of another order, the order of spirit.

The average individual still finds as much difficulty as did Nicodemus in thinking in terms of spirit. In the twelfth century Abelard said: 'The reign of the Father and the Son is ended; the reign of the Spirit is begun.' He was definitely premature, for while most people can give some significant content to the terms 'God the Father' and 'God the Son', 'God the Holy Ghost' remains a meaningless phrase until the individual is helped to become aware of the spiritual part of his own nature and to find that it is every bit as real as the instinctive part, and that it alone has power of freeing him from the instinctive, with which it comes 'into collision'.

'Collision' may seem a strange word to use in this connection, but it is not too strong a word to describe the experience by which the individual, despite great suffering and frustration, consciously chooses the way of advance into life rather than the way of self-pity and despair. In that moment 'the Spirit beareth witness with our spirit', and it is as if 'The edge of the self is touching a circle of life beyond itself to which it responds; the human heart is sensitive to God as the retina is to light waves'.⁷ A woman once described

151

the effect of a crushing blow as follows: 'I felt that I was sinking despairingly down into the blackness of a deep well. Suddenly everything changed, for I seemed to touch something which lifted my despair and gave me power to rise. I found I could go on again after all. I suppose one would call that something "God".'

I

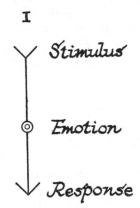

Stimulus

Emotion

Response

The alternative then to mere Stoicism on the one hand or flight from life on the other is faith in a larger life. But lest any should regard this as nothing but a form of dope, like anodyne for the pain of the body, let it be remembered that it is the way that took Christ to the Cross, Socrates to the hemlock, Bruno to the stake and Gandhi to the assassin's dagger. Such experiences are not for the average man, but they give the answer to the charge that religion is nothing but escapism.

The religious way is not a way that can be learnt about through the head; it requires humility, in the best sense of that word, and courage, for it must be tried in experience, as the parachute had to be tried by somebody brave enough to jump. Once tested, however, goodness receives a new and a creative content.

Perhaps the long process of development from the 'freedom' of unfettered impulsive action to the more difficult freedom of the spirit can be illumined with a few simple diagrams. In impulsive action, response follows stimulus without reflection and with little emotional tone save the pleasure that accompanies satisfied desire (Diagram I).

When, however, the child's immediate response is for any reason considered undesirable, the average adult will try to provide an alternative satisfaction which meets the same need of sensory experience. It may be something as simple as substituting a rattle for the father's watch, and the 'sublimation' may work if handled with sufficient skill. As the child

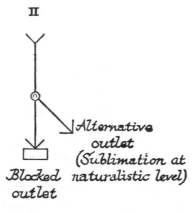

II

Alternative
outlet
(Sublimation at
Blocked naturalistic level)
outlet

grows the process becomes more complex and demands more skill from the educator and a certain willingness to be co-operative on the part of the child. The dominating bully may have to be helped to find an outlet for his aggression in a position which still requires his leadership, but on what Adler calls 'the useful side', so that society may be spared one more dictator (Diagram II). Such an attempt at sublimation will only work if the alternative outlet offered is of the same type as the one denied in the sense that it 'coheres' with the same instinctive need. Satisfactory alternatives become increasingly difficult to find as life advances and the child, adolescent or adult who has never learnt to accept some deprivations with courage is in for a hard time. He is also going to give his associates a hard time when, as is sooner or later inevitable, he runs into the situation represented by Diagram III. For here all avenues are barred to the satisfaction of his need. There is no outlet, no answer, no conceivable solution, no acceptable substitute for what is denied.

III

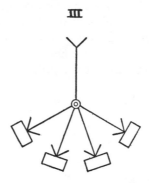

No available outlet

What happens then? Glib talk of sublimation is futile to one who finds himself in such an impasse, and an insult to one with a broken heart.

There are three alternatives before the sufferer: (1) Escape, which, whether it takes place on the physical or mental

IV

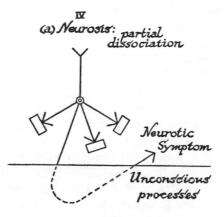

(a) Neurosis: partial dissociation

Neurotic Symptom

Unconscious processes

154

plane, is a form of suicide, of self destruction, quick or slow.

Diagrams IV and V illustrate the mechanisms whereby the individual may seek to escape from his suffering by the unconscious device of neurosis or psychosis. In the former, the distressing fact is 'forgotten'; put away behind an Iron Curtain or into an oubliette. But though forgotten, it does not die or remain inactive, but lives on and expresses itself in a circuitous manner, through some form of compulsive or obsessional behaviour, such as agarophobia or hysteria, which is beyond the control of the individual and causes a seepage of his energies.

In the latter, the psychosis, the dissociation from the painfully toned complex is more complete and the task of recovering contact with it and assimilating it to conscious processes, correspondingly more difficult.

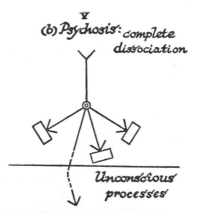

V
(b) Psychosis: complete dissociation

Unconscious processes

The second alternative confronting frustrated emotions is the way of endurance. Stoic courage is admirable, but as we have seen, it is not enough. To remain in the condition represented by Diagram III may be precarious if all joy and meaning have gone from life. Shakespeare has given us the picture of Viola heroically 'smiling at grief' and not asking for pity:

155

'She never told her love,
But let concealment like a worm i' the bud
Feed on her damask cheek.'

But the forces behind the unlived life are not going to be permanently satisfied with such a barren, if brave, 'solution'. They will not be denied until they are recognised and integrated. They will destroy us, as a plant deprived of light and sun is destroyed, unless they can be given new direction in the light of new vision.

The last diagram illustrates the possibility of such a process, of an alchemy whereby the inhibited forces and hungers of the natural self may be taken up, and transmuted

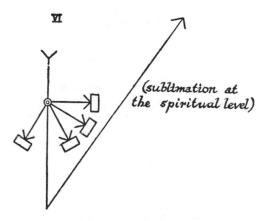

(sublimation at the spiritual level)

into new life by the spiritual self. Such an alchemy presupposes a belief, or at least a willingness to entertain the hypothesis, that life as we normally know it is not all there is to be known; that there is Light beyond, and that our destiny, even in the darkness, is ever to grow towards that Light; that just as new life can spring from the fallen seed, so can new birth arise from the ashes of our hopes, and that there is another power available to us to reinforce our endeavour, a power that can lift the mind out of its fatal tendency to harden and drift back on itself; a power that can enable us to achieve new levels of consciousness, new insight and perception. This is called the power of the spirit.

How can this creative attitude be built up in one who is broken in mind and spirit? How can faith in life be renewed, and the willingness to act as if life has meaning be stimulated in one who feels profoundly convinced that everything is futile? To such questions the psychotherapist would give a great deal to know the answer, for then his work of healing would be comparatively straightforward.

But, of course, there is no such thing as 'the' answer. Many techniques are being tried and many more will doubtless be proposed in the years to come. Perhaps, basic to all others, is the forming of an affective relationship to someone who is wise and kind and at the same time a 'window-opener'; one who has the capacity of enabling others to see the far distances that he himself has seen. In addition, sometimes the realisation that there are others needing one's help; or the practice of an art that reveals new and unsuspected wonders and relationships will inspire sufficient valour in the broken or frustrated individual to revive in him the capacity for effort. No one can tell what may be the nature of the inciting moment for any particular person. It may be a combination of several different things. What is certain is that willingness to try the untrodden path, to take a chance on finding meaning, needs courage, detachment from self-pity and heroic perseverance. Moreover, the path being both steep and narrow, the faint-hearted and those of feeble vision—and that means well nigh all of us—will need constant reassurance that it does lead somewhere. To few is it given to know such vivid experiences of the 'not-self' as St. Joan knew through her Voices, Teresa through her visions, Socrates through his Daimon; but all who have not closed their minds can receive intimations of 'the Beyond that is within', of a Presence that accompanies us as we tread the wine-press. And to all who faithfully seek will come at least some degree of conviction that the life we now know through the senses is not all that there is to be known. Reason alone can tell us nothing of these things, though in themselves they are not unreasonable. But where reason fails, humility and quiet listening can succeed.

But just as when, on the physical level, we wish to acquire a new skill, we must not try too hard, but must learn to stand aside, to get our surface selves out of the way and let things happen, to combine close attention with non-action in the mood of alert passivity or attentive calm, so also on the spiritual plane, we must not want too much or strive too intensely, for 'It is not we who make the gale of inspiration blow for us . . . we simply receive the gale, consent to its motion and let our ship sail under it, not hindering it by our resistance'.[8]

On the naturalistic level we saw that goodness requires that we keep the rules of our society and try to implement the values to which we subscribe. We saw that this could only be done when we have sufficient self-knowledge to make integrated functioning possible; when we operate as whole, not as fragmented individuals—in short, that integration is essential to integrity. But for those awakened to the realisation that spiritual power can in fact break through into consciousness, goodness takes on a new aspect and significance. In the cogent words of William Law: 'The difference between a good man and a bad man does not lie in this, that the one wills that which is good and the other does not, but solely in this, that the one concurs with the living, inspiring spirit of God within him, and the other resists it, and can be chargeable with evil only because he resists it.'

Goodness in this religious sense means more than keeping the law as an integrated individual; it means active and positive co-operation with what we conceive to be the will of God. It means relating the natural to the supernatural.

CHAPTER X

FROM THE AUTHORITARIAN APPROACH TO THE INWARD: I. IN EDUCATION

You go outside for assistance and that is just what you should not do. No one can really advise you or help you. The only way is to have recourse to yourself. Ask yourself why you write; try to find out whether the roots of it are planted in your heart of hearts.

RAINER MARIA RILKE: Letter to a young poet.

THE GOAL OF ALL education is growth towards fuller maturity. Our society is more concerned with this goal than ever before, since it is now in real danger of extinction as a result of its immaturity. Events of recent decades, particularly the rise of secular 'religions' of Fascism and Communism, have awakened the thoughtful to a realisation of the fact that the majority of people, no matter what their age, do not grow up, do not become self-directing. Psychologists are constantly producing studies[1] on the nature of maturity and immaturity; on why some like to dominate, others to obey; why some like to manage, others to be managed; or why one and the same person may alternate between authoritarianism and docility.

In his book, *All Hallows' Eve*, Charles Williams gives a vivid and terrifying picture of how easily the power-loving mind can gain control over the obsequious and grateful masses. The picture is reminiscent of the Nuremberg Rallies, and both pictures receive psychological support from the analytic findings of Freud, who tells us that man's inner irresolution, his reliance on others and his craving for authority cannot be exaggerated.

What can education do in the face of such an alarming verdict? In the past there have been enthusiasts who were sure it could do everything. After World War I, H. G. Wells asserted that civilisation was now a race between education and catastrophe. Catastrophe won, and in the light of that bitter failure our optimism is considerably chastened and our claims more modest. But there is no need to go to the extreme of despair, for the race is not yet over. Education may not be able to do everything, but it can certainly do a great deal, depending on the wisdom and maturity of the educator.

For education is not, as the common use of the word implies, a finished article; something you 'get' from school as you get an inoculation from the clinic. It is a continuous and a lifelong process, and there is no such thing yet as an educated person. Neither is education merely a matter of degree, of learning ever more and more. There is a qualitative aspect to it which is a good deal more important than the quantitative.

The 'free schools', as they are called, have realised this and have tried to shift the emphasis from instruction of the intellect to development of the whole child; from teaching subjects to tracing the relationships between subjects; from competitive success to the cultivation of good emotional attitudes. In consequence, they have been accused, and with some justice, of falling down on the intellectual side of education, a side which has hitherto been valued more highly than the emotional, because it is more easily measurable. To maintain a balance between all aspects of life, neglecting none, is a difficult task, but it is certainly right to try to redress the over-intellectualisation that has landed us with more knowledge than we know how to handle with safety.

Another criticism of the free schools is that they do not know where to draw the line between freedom and licence, that they over-reacted from the past emphasis on order, to a state of confusion in which nobody can possibly learn anything. Certainly education cannot take place in an atmosphere of confusion where everyone follows the whim of the moment, any more than it can take place in the atmosphere of a beehive or by the methods of the drill sergeant. 'No; my child would not like all this chaos and untidiness at all' decided one prospective parent. 'It's so messy,' commented another. Yes; education for democracy is rather messy. It follows no clearly defined road, only a general direction. It has to steer its way between the Scylla of liberty and the Charybdis of order; it has to prepare children for life in the world as it is, and to that extent must be traditional in its methods; and it has to encourage them to think in terms of a changing world without being superior about it, and without suggesting that 'we in the free schools know all the answers'. For, of course, experiments in freedom are not confined to a few pioneer schools, but are taking place, quietly and unnoticed, in many a school not labelled 'progressive'. Moreover, there have been educational reformers through the ages, and those of to-day should say with Lord Kelvin: 'If I have seen further than other men, it is because I have been standing on the shoulders of giants.'

All men would agree that, theoretically speaking, freedom is good, but unfortunately the word is as vague and equivocal as the word 'love' unless it is related to specific situations, so that we know exactly what we are talking about and can answer such questions as: Freedom for whom and under what conditions? How much freedom? Freedom from what? Freedom for what?, etc. For freedom also is not an isolated thing or an unlimited thing like sunshine, of which we can have all we will without shortening the supply for others and without blocking our own freedoms in other directions. It is therefore more useful to speak of specific freedoms than of freedom in general.

Keeping to the sphere of education, let us ask the first question: Freedom for whom? A raw recruit once gave the impulsive answer, 'For everybody, of course,' an answer that recalls the elephant cheerfully declaiming 'Each for himself and God for us all as he danced among the chickens.' Unlimited freedom for everybody in every department of life is an obvious impossibility, since freedoms, like loyalties, 'cut up against one another'. From the nursery school onwards, the needs and desires of one clash with those of another, and it requires much wisdom to work out solutions that will be acceptable to all concerned, whether the conflicts centre round four- or forty-year-olds, whether the scene of action is the nursery school or the United Nations Assembly.

There are however certain situations where a high degree of freedom should be possible for all, as, for example, in classroom discussions on relatively impersonal topics. It has been claimed that 'In the American Protestant culture, perhaps the most significant influence upon religious development is the fact that youth is normally encouraged to question authority. He is expected, if not by his family, at least by his college and his contemporaries, to scrutinise critically all established ways of looking at things. He is not only permitted, but actively encouraged, to find flaws in the school, in the home, in the social system, in the Church.'[2] Such freedom of thought and discussion is common to all colleges in democratic countries, and long may it remain so. Unfortunately, education is often controlled by those who hold a contrary viewpoint—namely, that since 'we know what's right', it is therefore our duty to teach it and not allow the young to become confused by being exposed to other points of view. If such controllers get their way, freedom of discussion might be curtailed or forbidden in those academic circles which have enjoyed it for so long that they take it for granted. For it is clear that, though all men do lip service to the word 'freedom', many would only allow it in the spheres that they approve of, such as business enterprise on the one hand or State control on the other; freedom to be a Protestant in Elizabethan England, freedom to be a Catholic in modern Spain. Few can sincerely say with Voltaire: 'I disagree with everything you say, but I will fight to the death for your right to say it.' Indeed, the Archbishop of Seville, Cardinal Segura, has recently remarked: 'It causes one real pain to see the tolerance shown to the non-Catholic sects amongst us.'

The second question, Freedom from what? receives a strangely interesting answer in Eric Fromm's recent study, *Escape from Freedom*. Why should anyone wish to escape from so excellent a thing as freedom? Yet, under certain circumstances, they do. Witness the poet's lament:

'Me this unchartered freedom tires,
I feel the weight of chance desires.'

Or the complaint of the small child who, on arrival at his 'free' school one morning, asked sadly: 'Do we have to do what we want to-day? Can't we do what you tell us?'

This second question cannot properly be discussed apart from the third and the fourth. Freedom from freedom is only craved by immature adults who have never learned to direct their own lives, and by children overwhelmed with too much choice before their knowledge and interests are sufficiently developed to give them the capacity for selection and rejection. Therefore there are occasions when to give too much freedom can be just as mistaken as to give too little. We have seen that children need guidance as well as freedom in the early 'tribal' stages of development. The educator also needs guidance in knowing when and how much to give of one or of the other, and for this he must rely mainly on an experienced intuition and on skill in the practice of timeliness.

One thing that can definitely be said is that freedom of action is less important than freedom of thought and feeling. Children tolerate a very astonishing amount of restriction in the sphere of action without any serious damage resulting therefrom, provided their thoughts and feelings are free.

The questions 'freedom from what?' and 'for what?' are interrelated and interdependent, as illustrated by the truism, 'You can't have it both ways'. We must decide what we want most and be willing to pay the price. If we want freedom to be a proficient musician, artist, poet or lover, certain renunciations will be necessary, certain disciplines have to be undertaken. The impulse of the moment will sometimes have to be sacrificed to the long-term goal. This is as true in the realm of religion as of art. Those who would achieve 'The glorious liberty of the children of God' must sacrifice the liberty of the instinctual. Attachment to the higher involves detachment from the lower when the lower gets in the way. Greed, possessiveness, pride and power-hunger have to give way to make room for the larger good. The freedom of the spirit is dependent on freedom from control by the instinctive; attachment to means detachment from. This is the meaning of the Prayer Book phrase, 'Whose service is perfect freedom'. Merely to renounce, merely to chasten the life of instinct unless a higher good is seen to make such detachment desirable, is mistaken and futile asceticism. The instinctive life is like a power-house; good and necessary, but to be kept under control. For the artist in living, the pattern is exactly the same as for the artist in any particular department of life. Freedom for creativity means freedom from those fears and passions and ambitions that hinder creativity.

The problem facing the educator therefore is not in the form of a choice between alternatives. It is not a problem of 'which shall we have in this school, freedom or authority?' Thinking in absolutes only lands us in trouble, because life is very complex. The problem is rather how to blend freedom and authority in such wise proportions that the child gets the guidance and control necessary to him without restriction of his capacity for enterprise in the field of thought, feeling or action. For this discrimination there are no rule-of-thumb directions to be followed; like all of education, it is a fine art.

Because there is a place for authority as well as for freedom in education, that does not mean there is also a place for authoritarianism. The distinction should be kept clear, and we need to be constantly on guard against the danger of letting the one degenerate into the other, against letting the impersonal prohibition, 'You cannot do that', degenerate into 'You learn to obey me and do as I say because I say so'. The authoritarian personality enjoys his use of power over others: the genuine educator tries to help the child achieve power over himself. But it is well to remember that here too there are no pure distinctions, that most if not all of us have a trace of power-lust, and that one and the same individual may be docile and obedient to his superiors, but tyrannical to his inferiors. From studies that have been made into the mentality of pre-war Germany, this would appear to have been very much the case, especially in the Army.

A teacher or parent who could not wield authority as the occasion demanded would soon be in difficulties. But whereas the aim of the true educator is always to further the growth of the child and to hasten the day when he will no longer need the authority or guidance of another, the authoritarian is concerned with imposing 'right' thinking and behaviour according to his own standards and beliefs, of which he can tolerate neither question nor criticism. The aim of the first is creative growth in an atmosphere of ordered freedom; the aim of the second is uniformity of thought and behaviour in an atmosphere of unquestioning obedience.

We might perhaps say that it is only safe to use authority when we ourselves are free from authoritarianism, but the sorry fact is that we often think we are free when in fact we are not; or we may be free from it in one sphere and not in another. A fervent opponent of political intolerance once angrily remarked of his wife: 'Mary will have to think as I do if we are going to be happy together.' And a very advanced free-thinker remarked to a sympathetic friend: 'One thing would break me: if Philip (his seven-year-old son) ever wanted to become a Christian.' Both quoted

Voltaire and regarded themselves as his disciples. But they were living 'in their heads' and failing to relate their theories to their own actual feelings and behaviour. We are not saved from our emotional prejudices and egocentricities by virtue of belonging to the intelligentsia of the twentieth century, and unless we are on the alert, 'love of freedom' can slip into the attitude of 'I have a right to my opinion and you have a right to my opinion'.[3] We may laugh at the unconscious slip of the minister who took farewell of his opponent with the kindly words, 'Ah, well. We are both serving the same God; you in your way and I in His,' and yet ourselves be capable of the same attitude. The great Thomas Huxley once turned on his antagonist with the crushing comment: 'You mistake me; my desire to prove the truth of this matter is as nothing compared with my desire for your extermination.' He was joking, and yet his words indicate the strength of the passion to be admitted right which exists in all of us.

Therefore parents, teachers, spiritual pastors and masters 'and all those set in authority' need to remember continuously that the price of remaining humble, tentative and related, while at the same time fulfilling the requirements of firm and effective administration, is 'eternal vigilance', since authoritarianism can so easily creep up on us, or live on in us, without our conscious awareness, and in opposition to our professed ideals.

And while keeping watch over ourselves, we must also constantly watch and study our children. A new and revolutionary approach came into education with the teachings of that 'Copernicus of pedagogy', Rousseau. Some of those teachings were superficial and are open to challenge, but no one who wants to find the truth of things has ever challenged his basic directive: *Étudiez donc bien vos enfants, car très assurement vous ne les connaient point.*' This was a complete *volte-face* from the current authoritarianism of the time, when people thought they knew, either from the authority of Holy Writ, or from their own divinely inspired intuition, the nature and needs, and therefore the right treatment of, the child. John Locke 'knew' that the mind at birth was a *tabula rasa,* or wax tablet, on which the adult could make what impressions he pleased. Susannah Wesley, like many others, 'knew' that the child was born in sin, and that therefore the parents' first duty was to break the child's will, not only that he might be manageable in this life, but for the still more urgent reason (or rationalisation) that 'The parent who indulges his child's will does the devil's work, makes religion impracticable, salvation unattainable; and does all that in him lies to damn his child, soul and body, for ever'. Poor Mrs. Wesley! As mother of nineteen children, she certainly needed a theory of character education that would ensure some peace and quiet in the home, or, as Dr. MacTaggart said of eternal punishment, 'No human constitution could stand it'. She had good enough excuse for being somewhat authoritative without the need of such a fantastic theology to cover her severity.

The genetic and scientific approach advocated by Rousseau requires us to rid our minds of authoritarian and of private views of human nature and to examine that nature with the same openness of mind that we should bring to any other branch of scientific study. If we do this we find in the child, not a *tabula rasa,* or a man in miniature, or a limb of Satan, or an angel of light, but a complex organism, capable of indefinite growth, with many needs and impulses, some of which will conflict. For example, in reference to the matter of authority, we find that whereas in infancy and childhood the exercise of authority may have seemed a relatively simple matter, with the dawn of adolescence it becomes exceedingly complicated. The child now 'can't wait to grow up'. He longs to be self-supporting and to be emancipated from the restraints of parental control; yet he also still wants security and guidance. He demands the right to think for himself and yet is irritated by what seems to him a lack of guidance from his parents, and he takes pride in those parents if they show that they know what's what. Such remarks as 'My Mom brings us up right' and

'My mother doesn't allow us to do that' (spoken with approval) demonstrate a need to feel firm ground beneath them in the realm of moral behaviour. And yet all the time the desatellisation process goes on, or should go on, for the youth should be finding new centres of security and loyalty outside the home which will further the process of 'emancipation' from his parents. If the standards of his 'peer groups' differ from those of his parents, he will feel critical of the latter, and guilty because of his criticism.

As a result of these ambivalent feelings, of wanting to love and to criticise at the same moment, conflict is inevitable. It is, moreover, lifelong, since neither complete freedom nor complete security is attainable in this life, nor complete wisdom in parents. The parent, therefore, has a well-nigh impossible task—a good reason for not undertaking parenthood lightly. He must be flexible, yet firm; moral, yet not moralistic; protective and loving, yet willing to let his child grow, and eventually to 'lose' him; ready to give guidance, yet never imposing it at the adolescent stage, save in the very rare situations which may justify him. How successfully he does all this, especially through the stormy 'teen-age' period, will depend on his own level of maturity and on the soundness of the personality structure he has helped the child build up in the earliest years. If a wise and reasonable use of freedom has been made all along the line; if freedom has been graduated in relation both to the child's temperament and to his stage of growth, then it should be possible to avoid the production of adults who seek to escape from freedom on the one hand or from authority on the other. As an example of the former would be the child who, when confronted by her mother with a choice of action, said meekly: 'I want to do what Mother wants me to do.' The mother was pleased, not realising the danger to the child's personality development in such docility and refusal of independence. An example of the latter would be the European boys, who, on arrival in America, said: 'Good. Now we can do what we please. This is a free country.'

To steer a middle course and keep the balance between extremes is no easy task. In trying to avoid one mistake, we all too readily tend to over-react into its opposite for we assume that the opposite of the bad must be good. Rousseau, for all his remarkable insight, was guilty of advocating this over-reaction when he gave the foolish advice: 'Do the opposite of what is generally done, and you will do the right thing.' How simple that rule would make life; and how mechanical. But life is not mechanical; it is organic, and therefore education must be the same, especially education in virtue. The Sunday school teacher who put on the black-board a list of 'Things Jesus does not like' was making two mistakes: firstly, her concept of virtue was that it consisted solely in avoiding certain forms of bad behaviour which were as unrelated to each other as beads on a string. Secondly, her concept was authoritarian. She was not helping children to think for themselves, explore their own feelings in relation to concrete situations and to each other according to their ability. She was saying in effect: 'These things are wrong because Jesus does not like them' and for no other reason. Certainly virtue may be nourished and strengthened by the inspiration of great example whether of Jesus or another; but unless children are helped to discover that they them-selves do not like these things—stealing, lying, or whatever— then it will be that much harder for them to achieve self-direction, and to act from the authority of their own inner centre and conviction. They will be more likely to go through life asking someone else to tell them what is right and how to behave.

In this sphere more than any other there is a great gulf fixed between instruction and education, a gulf of which the 'man in the street' is sadly unaware. It is still generally supposed that virtue can be taught, verbally and authorita-tively. Virtue cannot be taught; it can only be learnt by increasing self-understanding and applying words to experi-ence.

The sixteen-year-old boy who recently shot a policeman

said it made him feel big, 'like in the movies'. He had been taught the Seventh Commandment, but he had certainly not learnt to relate it to his own undisciplined, instinctive drives. Actually, it is doubtful if he so much wanted to kill as to feel big and powerful. For one in his rudimentary stage of emotional control, he had certainly been allowed too much freedom in the use of firearms.

It should surely be a platitude by now that the education of the emotional life is a difficult, complex and lifelong process which no doctrinal teaching can short-circuit. Another mistaken dictum of Jean Jacques Rousseau was that 'Everything is good as it comes from the hands of the Creator; everything degenerates in the hands of man', the implication being that children would be all right if we did not interfere with them. On this point, the man in the street knows better, but the Rousseauesque theorist is still among us. 'It was assumed that if you were given freedom, you would behave well', was the sad and naïve comment of one disillusioned teacher to children guilty of breaking the rules which they themselves had made. There is nothing in psychological teaching to justify this assumption, and nearly two thousand years ago St. Paul showed truer insight when he said, with courageous honesty, 'What I find then is this. . . . I agree happily with the law of God in my inner self, but I find another law at work in my bodily organs, a law at war with my reason.'

Yet the so-called 'free' school is right in its distaste for authoritarianism and for the imposition of 'good' behaviour by the use of superior power and/or by mechanical verbal teaching. 'Nobody tells us what's right,' remarked a girl of ten in one such school. She may merely have been stating a fact or she may have had just ground for complaint in that she was getting insufficient guidance, but at least the school was right in holding that children should think out behaviour problems for themselves as far as possible. The mistake such schools often make is the mistake of Socrates—that

'Knowledge is virtue'. It is hard enough to know what is right, but, alas! knowing is not enough. Doing it is something else. One might question the first line of Drinkwater's poem, but one must agree with the second:

'Knowledge we ask not; knowledge Thou hast sent;
But Lord the will, there lies our bitter need.'[4]

In the sphere of religion above all others, we should avoid being dictatorial. An authoritarian Protestant minister said angrily to the youth of his flock venturing to explore a Catholic Church: 'You cannot expect a blessing if you go there.' With such a bigoted outlook let us contrast two parents of religious but non-sectarian outlook who encouraged their adolescent children to visit different churches, and discussed with them afterwards what they found interesting and valuable in the one or the other. Or let us contrast the attitude expressed in the following lines in which the mother's concern is that her son should do his own growing and find, not her way, but his, realising that no religious truth could be his which he had not found for himself; that, in the words of George Macdonald, 'Each generation must do its own seeking and finding. The father's having found is only the warrant for the children's search.'

To My Son

I will not say to you: This is the Way,
walk in it. For I do not know your way
                or where the Spirit may lead you.

        It may be
to paths I never trod, or ships by the sea
leading to unimagined lands far,
                or, haply, to a star.

Or yet again
through dark and perilous places, racked with pain and full
  of fear
your road may lead you. Far from me or near,
    I cannot guess or guide
    but only stand aside.

    Just this I'll say;
I know for very truth there is a Way
for each to walk, a Right for each to choose,
    a Truth to use.

And, though you wander far, your soul will know that true
  path when you find it.
    Therefore, go!
I will fear nothing for you day or night.
I will not grieve at all because your light is called by some
  new name—
    Truth is the same.
It matters nothing to call it Star or Sun!
    All light is one.[5]

CHAPTER XI

FROM THE AUTHORITARIAN
APPROACH TO THE INWARD:
II. IN RELIGION

Authoritarianism in the religious life is . . . the search for criteria
of truth in a lower world to serve the purposes of a higher one.
It is the attempt to draw from the natural world the standards
of the spiritual world, a process which shows that the ultimate
ground of confidence is exterior rather than the interior, belonging to the constraint of what is natural rather than the liberty of
what is spiritual.

NICOLAS BERDYAEV: Freedom and the Spirit.

'You make it all so difficult' is the criticism often
levelled by the unquestioning believer at those who try to
seek out the inner meanings of religion. The implication is
that there is no need for this exploring, that religion is a
matter of simple faith, and it is therefore not only unnecessary but mistaken to apply one's intellect to it.

What is the explanation of the gap that so often exists
between maturity in years and maturity in religious thought
and feeling? A frequently offered explanation is that 'Most
people like to have their thinking done for them', but this
is not wholly true, for many people who prefer not to think
about their religion think quite independently and effectively
in other spheres.

Perhaps part of the answer lies in a certain dislocation in
our emotional development. Life has forced us to grow up
faster than we wanted to in so many directions, that in self

protection we keep one area where we can remain emotionally infantile without disapproval from anybody. There are other more pressing matters to think about. We have to struggle through exams, to choose and train for a career, to fight for our country, to find a job and pull our weight in it, to support a family and make ends meet, to care for our children and help them with their problems as well as our own; to wrestle with illness, fatigue and constant disappointment. Is it any wonder that an unconscious or half-conscious impulse pleads, 'Let us at least keep one sphere where we can relax and sing "Peace, perfect peace" if we feel like it'?

If we take an inward look at ourselves, we do not need modern psychology to tell us that the infant lives on in the adult, continuing its cry for comfort, security, protection. Few of us seem to have had sufficient of these things in childhood, and even for those who had, life remains a difficult, precarious and an alarming business. 'Let me to thy bosom fly' is a very natural human plea.

And why not? There is Biblical support for the attitude: 'Comfort ye, comfort ye my people, saith your God. Speak ye comfortably to Jerusalem.' And did not Jesus offer rest and easy yoke to His followers? Yes, assuredly we all need some degree of comfort if we are to cope with life satisfactorily and stay on an even keel. But the original meaning of that term *con forte* was 'with strength'. Jesus relieved people's sufferings, but He did not, like Father Simon,[1] invite them to revert to infantility to become obedient 'insects'. 'Take my yoke upon you and learn,' is an exhortation to active effort, not to the supine passivity of that type of pseudo-religion described not altogether untruthfully as 'the opium of the people'.

In Hindu teaching, the name *tamas* is given to the 'conserving' aspect of our natures that tries to hold us back in a state of effortless inertia. This backward pull is necessary as a fulcrum, but it must be balanced against the stimulus and the inspiration of *sattwa*, i.e. the vision of what we would

like to do; and the force of *rajas*, i.e. the will power to conquer our lethargy and go forward and do it, to 'fight the
good fight'.

In this 'triangle of forces' each is essential to the other;
any one alone would be useless. Our problem is that of
keeping a balance between them. If one is over-emphasised
at the expense of the others, there will be serious disturbance
and perhaps a breakdown. For example, we hear a great deal
to-day, and rightly, about the need for security in the little
child, for we now know that where early security is lacking
it is not easily possible for imagination, inspiration (*sattwa*),
or the adventurous spirit and will (*rajas*) to develop. The
more probable development will be a neurotic demand for
100 per cent. security before any step is taken, so that there
can be no risk whatever. But life requires us to be adventurous, and on occasion to be willing to take a risk. The
tamas of 'Let me hide myself in thee' must be balanced by
the *rajas* of 'Onward, Christian soldiers'. 'I want a hide-out,'
moaned one weary pilgrim, but there is 'no place to hide',
no escape from the fact that life is a vigorous and unrelenting
process which requires us to accept our share of knocks and
deprivations, to get up and go on. We can and should, of
course, be sympathetic with those who, having had more
than their share, long only for cessation like the old woman
in the workhouse who sighed thankfully with her last
breath: 'I'm going to do nothing for ever and ever.' The
frequency of the tombstone epitaph 'At Rest' indicates how
widespread is this attitude. But such yearning for escape is a
sorry commentary on the imbalance of our lives, and we
must admit that neither a religion based on a weary longing
for rest nor a religion that is a phantasy compensation for
inadequate love and protection in early life can be called a
mature religion.

The most serious form of early insecurity is not caused by
poverty but by unsatisfactory personal relationships. Poverty
of material goods can be very harmful, but there is a form of
poverty that is worse. The child who has never felt love

175

and security in the sheltering arms of his parents, or the child who has had to leave that shelter before he was ready for such psychic weaning, will go through life emotionally starved, searching always for some 'illegitimate' equivalent of the love he never had in adequate supply. Unless and until he becomes conscious of what happened to him, wise enough to forgive it, and courageous enough to accept the scars of his deprivation and to go forward in spite of his maimed condition, then he will never be free from his infantile needs, and will remain in consequence an easy prey of the needs of others, especially of the power-hungry. The connection of this psychological condition with authoritarianism lies in the fact that it is easy for the dictator to win power over those who are wearily hungering for security and protection. Recent history has given a terrible lesson as to what can happen when people are willing to sacrifice selfhood for protective care and relief from anxiety.

Closely allied to this hunger for permanent parental care and the cessation of suffering is the hunger for certainty. The more immature the 'religious' group, the more certain it is that it has found 'the truth', and that no one can be saved who does not share the group's concept and representation of truth. And just as in totalitarian politics there is nothing further to discuss once the truth as to how the world ought to be run has been revealed and inscribed in political scriptures, so the religious fundamentalists—Bible Christians, Christadelphians, members of the Lord's Day Observance Society, Four Square Gospellers or Seventh Day Adventists and Revivalists generally—all 'know' God's plans for his universe, and those plans are above discussion for they too have been 'revealed'.

The laughable stupidity of such a claim would be obvious if our minds were less at the mercy of our emotional needs. 'The sectarian thinks that he has the whole sea ladled into his own little pond', but how can the growing, groping and imperfect human mind know the full and final truth in religion or any other sphere? The fundamentalist who

176

believes all answers are to be found between the covers of his Bible should contemplate the words written there: 'We know in part' and 'We see through a glass darkly'.

The claim that complete knowledge is possible for the 'elect' is foolish and arrogant and conducive to the authoritarian type of personality. Authoritarianism works in two directions and involves two complementary attitudes, both equally deplorable; the didactic and the gullible; the fascistic and the submissive. There could be no *führers* if there were none willing and wanting to be ordered and led. The mental inertia of *tamas* in the average individual offers a strong temptation to the dictator mind, and he will exploit it for his own power-loving ends wherever he can. It is therefore the business of the educator to discourage credulity and obsequious obedience, and to encourage a critical and enquiring, though humble, attitude of mind. We cannot afford to be complacent and say: 'Why worry about what people believe? Religion is a private matter, and if people like to worship a vengeful Jahveh, let them; that's their affair.' Unfortunately, that is not true. Much as we may wish to ignore the fact, we are social animals, and so are all involved in each other's thinking and feeling. The way others conceive of God may lead by hidden paths to very astonishing and terrifying results for ourselves. If God is 'a very vengeful gentleman indeed', as He was to the inmates of Fort Leavenworth, the Kansas penitentiary, then vengefulness receives an implicit approval. If He is so powerful that He can do what He likes, even contradicting His own moral laws of goodness and mercy, then sovereign power is evidently so good in itself as to be above criticism. This belief is actually held by some people: 'It shows God's sovereignty' was the explanation offered by one 'Bible Christian' to a child puzzled at the severity of the punishment meted out to all mankind because of one man's disobedience.

Instead, therefore, of enquiring of another, 'Do you believe in God?' it would be more pertinent to ask: 'In what

sort of a God do you believe? What is your concept of God?'
For there is a world of difference between a glorified tribal
chieftain who uses his despotic power quite ruthlessly on
those who disobey or displease him and the immanent
divine Spirit who awaits our response to His presence and
our co-operation with His purpose. Yet the same word,
'God', is used for both concepts, as the following dialogue
illustrates:

Roger Lyons, the Director of religious programmes for
the Voice of America, was rumoured to be an atheist, so he
went before Senator McCarthy for an investigation, which
went as follows:

McCarthy: You do not claim to belong to any religious
group?

Lyons: I do not.

McC.: How would you describe yourself? Would you
describe yourself as an atheist, agnostic, a Christian or
Jewish?

Lyons: I am not an atheist or agnostic. I believe in God.

McC.: Do you think that a man who is in charge of
religious programming might do a better job if he belonged
to some Church himself and were a regular church-goer?

Lyons: Not necessarily. . . . We deal with areas of the world
that are largely Buddhist, Moslem, Hindu and so forth. . . .

Lyons went on to give an account of his training and
studies, including the study of psychology in Switzerland
under associates of the world-famed Carl Jung. McCarthy
promptly demanded: 'This Professor Jung, does he not go to
any church or synagogue?'

Lyons: I don't know.'[2]

One is inevitably reminded of the trial and death of
Socrates. This great teacher though accused of impiety, also
believed in God, but not in the same tribal god or gods as
his accusers, not in an autocratic Deity who demanded that
we attend church and ask no disturbing questions.

Man makes his anthropomorphic god or gods in his own
image and to correspond to his own emotional needs. If,

like Hitler, he hungers for power, then the only god he can admire, if any, will also be a powerful autocrat. If he is dependent and needs to be led, he must also have a heavenly Dictator to lean upon. If he is neither the one nor the other, but a seeker, his god will be the spirit of truth that leads us into all truth.

It therefore behoves the educator and parent to become as aware as they can of the emotional needs both of themselves and their children, and to be on the watch to discourage authoritarian attitudes from both ends as it were, in the leader and the led, in the arrogant and the obsequious; for each encourages the tendency of the opposite. To look up to another quite uncritically is to invite him to become 'a little tin god', if nothing worse. The position of the pulpit and of the teacher's desk may be necessary, but both preacher and teacher should realise that that position offers a subtle temptation to the attitude and relationship of *de haut en bas*. They should watch for the tendency in themselves to make dogmatic utterances rather than to stimulate and clarify through free and frank discussion. The teacher can only teach effectively if he knows something of what is going on in the minds of his hearers, some of whom may be wiser than himself.

Those who believe in democratic rather than authoritarian methods should not only foster the spirit of free enquiry, but should avoid the language of emotional dependence. For example, Mr. Charles Morgan says of the Litany: 'It is wonderfully comprehensive. One would venture to say that there is no human need, spiritual or temporal, that is not remembered in it.'[3] Perhaps so, but one must also admit that many of these needs are expressed in language that is deplorably feudal and even cringing. To preserve beautiful and time-honoured language because it is beautiful is one thing, but it is regrettable if its literal usage causes the Church to be accused, and with justice, of officially endorsing and perpetuating a feudalistic or tribal conception of God. It must be admitted that the tone of such pleading as

'Remember not, Lord, our offences nor the offences of our forefathers, neither take thou vengeance on our sins: spare us, good Lord, spare Thy people whom Thou hast redeemed with Thy most precious blood, and be not angry with us for ever' is the tone of grovelling fear of an arbitrary, vengeful and unpredictible Potentate rather than of confident trust in a loving and merciful Father. The beauty of the music to which the words are sung cannot alter their significance. Why invite people to worship a 'god' so patently inferior to King Alfred, Marcus Aurelius or any of the good and great men that we know?

In 1928 the Church of England made a valiant but unsuccessful attempt to introduce a revised Prayer Book. Whether a Church ought not to be master in its own house and independent of a Parliamentary vote is not a matter for discussion here. What we can say is that the failure would not perhaps matter so much if people, instead of being exhorted from the pulpit to believe, were encouraged to think more for themselves. Loss of faith would be less common and might indeed be unknown if faith was built step by step on personal exploration and experience, rather than on the precarious foundation of authoritarian dictates. Personal building up of a religious approach to life does not, of course, mean that the religious authorities of the ages should be ignored or abandoned. On the contrary, we should learn gladly and gratefully from them as we are able. But if the individual subscribes to the doctrinal beliefs of others without testing them to discover whether they also reflect his own thought and feeling experience, then he is in danger of becoming incapable of independent religious thinking, or, if he suddenly wakes up and decides to think for himself, he may lose his faith along with his beliefs.

Man should know himself for what he truly is: a creature in process of becoming, one whose destiny is to co-operate consciously with the forces of his own evolution. He cannot thus co-operate if he remains for ever supinely expecting to be told what to think and do by an authority on earth or in

Heaven, begging to be led, protected, guided, forgiven and cared for by an all-powerful external deity dwelling 'on high'. Jung expresses these contrasting concepts in vivid terms: 'If I accept the fact that God is absolute, and beyond all human experience, He leaves me cold. . . . But if I know that God is a mighty activity within my soul, at once I must concern myself with Him.'[4] But with a feudal lord whose doubtful benevolence must be appealed to in such cringing terms as 'Lord, have mercy upon us', 'We beseech Thee to hear us, good Lord', 'Receive our humble petitions', 'Good Lord deliver us', and so on, my relationship will obviously be very different.

Some parts of the Prayer Book, and notably some of the collects, are expressions of such beauty and insight that they should no more be altered than should a Shakespeare sonnet. Even where the anthropomorphic concepts in the mind of the writer are no longer acceptable, the prayers can be interpreted at deeper levels, without being changed. But where the emphasis is on petitioning and placating, rather than on the inner change of character and consciousness necessary to spiritual growth, religion is held down to an infantile level at which man becomes alienated from his own powers. Instead of seeking to know the truth, the will of God, and then to co-operate with it as a mature individual, he tries to win favour with the Diety by utter and quite dishonest self-depreciation and self-denigration: 'All our righteousness is as filthy rags.' This attitude appears to visualise all good states of mind, all virtues, as being outside itself; and then begs for them as though they were isolated and complete things, in God's power to give or to withhold. It is another expression of the 'beads on a string' concept of ready-made virtues, with God holding the string. 'Give peace in our time, O Lord' suggests that we believe He could if He would give us this blessing, regardless of whether we have achieved the sort of mentality that makes peace possible.

Then, again, if the remembrance of our sins is really

grievous unto us, the burden of them intolerable, it is for us to get to work on them instead of continuing to provoke 'most justly the wrath and indignation of the Divine Majesty against us'. If children addressed their earthly father in similar vein, we should regard them as suffering from an exaggerated guilt complex and badly in need of psychological help. What sort of God is it who reserves the right to be wrathful and unforgiving while He tells us to be loving and merciful? Certainly not the God of the New Testament.

In its origin, Christianity was not an authoritarian religion. Where it has become so, it is the result of man's love of power on the one hand and his laziness and love of direction on the other. In so far as it is true that people do in fact 'like to have their thinking done for them', this should be recognised and discouraged as a dangerous condition. Jesus deplored the servile attitude. He repudiated the title 'Good Master' with the retort, 'Why callest thou Me good? None is good save one, that is God.' Men cling to Him for protection and salvation from they know not what, but He preferred them to exercise their own understanding and to find out for themselves the truth of the way He taught. It distressed Him when they could not, and He appears to have been surprised as well as distressed at the lack of insight in His own selected disciples. 'Are ye also without understanding?'

Having repudiated all wealth, power and position by which worldly men seek to impose their authority over others, He was a challenge to the normal, to the accepted culture pattern of that day and this. Men of position who did not like this disturbance of their customary way of thought and feeling issued a counter-challenge in the demand: 'By what authority doest Thou these things and who gave Thee this authority?' Jesus, knowing that minds so rigid and so accustomed to thinking in terms of hierarchical power could not begin to understand, did not try to answer, but gave them a baffling counter-question to puzzle over. So also when asked for specific advice on such matters as paying tribute to Caesar, keeping the Sabbath, fasting, adultery or wine-drinking; He gave no trite or categorical answers. He did not publish an encyclical or lay down the law. He made a penetrating comment which sent men away less sure of themselves and their motivations, but more thoughtful, and perhaps more kind. Such trenchant and stirring pronouncements as 'The Sabbath was made for man and not man for the Sabbath', 'Give Caesar what belongs to Caesar, give God what belongs to God', and 'Let the innocent among you cast the first stone at her' caused men to stop short and start thinking about real values instead of tribal and traditional ones.

Not that Jesus was at all time non-directive and non-committal. There were occasions when His meaning was intensively clear and times when His words stung like a whip-lash as He turned on the hypocrites, the self-righteous Pharisees, the exploiters of the old and weak, the defilers of the Temple and those who warped the development of little children. These incidents cannot be reconciled with the perfectionist concept of Jesus as at all times gentle, patient and loving, or with His own teaching on non-violence in word and deed. But one can recognise His unique greatness without holding a Christology that claims He was perfect man and perfect God. One can understand that from His inner integrity and His union with God, flowed a power that could be felt, a power of a totally different order from that which depends on external position and possessions.

On his arrival at Fort Leavenworth Prison, the young psychologist was told by the Governor: 'If you blunder in this place, only God can help you, I can't. . . . Either you've got what it takes or you haven't.'[5] What did it take to walk fearlessly among those two thousand sometimes desperate and dangerous men? It took this same kind of inner strength and power—strength that flows from integrity of motivation and from a selfless concern for and interest in others. 'It'll always be how they feel about the particular man,' explained one official. Had they felt this stranger to be in any way meretricious, insincere or sentimental, his influence as a psychologist among them, and perhaps his very life, would have been over. 'A criminal has a fanatical respect for quality and integrity but is merciless to the pretentious and the pseudo.'[6]

But it is not only the criminal who senses and responds to the courage of integrity. It was said of Jesus that 'The common people heard him gladly' (John vii. 46), and felt that 'Never man spake like this man' for 'He taught as one having authority and not as the scribes' (Matt. vii. 29). That is to say, they felt His teaching to be authentic, coming from inner knowledge, not from some second-hand source. So, 'They were astonished at His doctrine; for His word was with power' (Luke iv. 32). 'Thou hast the words of eternal life, so what is the good of going to anyone else?' asked Peter (John vi. 68).

Where this authenticity exists, 'Where words come out of the depth of truth',[7] they inevitably come with power, and they do not need the mask of authoritarianism, nor the trappings of wealth and position, nor the techniques of propaganda to give them support. One remark from Jesus will outlive the millions of words poured into a political campaign and the vapid speeches which have made many tons of newsprint. For 'We seek collective power because we are incapable of individual greatness. . . . We seek to be many because none of us is able to be properly one',[8] and we seek to derive support from the external to make up for our lack in the inward and spiritual.

It was said of the Hindu saint Ramakrishna that he sought none of the respect that a *guru* normally exacted from his *chelas*. 'He put himself on a level with his young disciples. He was their companion, their brother; he talked familiarly with them and without any trace of superiority. He felt that the words he spoke came through him rather than from him. Moreover, he felt that true instruction does not consist in inculcating doctrine but in communicating.'[9]

This spirit and attitude is the mark of all great religious

184

leaders, all great teachers, therapists, artists and true democrats. In fact, it is the mark of all men in any sphere of living who, having shed their own egocentricities and discovered their own creative centres, are able to believe in and to stimulate the creative forces in others. Such men are not afraid to have their authority challenged or tested, for they are not interested in the preservation of their own prestige, but only in establishing authentic contact with the spiritual centre of life.

Among religious groups, it is perhaps the Quakers or Friends who, more than any others in the Western world, have explicitly abandoned all authority save the spiritual authority of the Inner Light. This does not mean they reject Christianity as inwardly understood, for they regard Jesus as the supreme exponent and revelation of this truth— that God is within and that our life-task is to become the organs of that indwelling spirit.

Among educators, it is men like Froebel and Pestalozzi who will ever be remembered for removing the emphasis from the subject-matter to the child and for teaching the revolutionary truth that the child, like the plant, has his own entelechy in accordance with which, rather than with the preconceived authoritarian ideas of the adult, he must be allowed to grow and develop.

In the political sphere, men such as Thomas Jefferson, Abraham Lincoln and William Gladstone, in contrast with the doctrinaire fanatic, sought the well-being of all men, all parties, and all classes. Whereas the totalitarian mentality (which is to be found in all countries in varying degree) merely seeks to replace one dictatorship by another, the true democrat believes, not that all men are equal in endowment, but that all are equal in respect of their humanity, and should therefore be given every opportunity for realising their potential, however small it be and whatever the cost in patience and apparent confusion. The authoritarian mind, whether in parent, teacher or politician, is more concerned with order, efficiency and uniformity than with individual development and growth towards maturity. Moreover, he cannot risk allowing people to think for themselves lest his own authority be challenged.

In the sphere of psychotherapy, this same principle of self-help and inner growth is universally recognised. The movement known as non-directive or client-centred counselling inspired and initiated by Dr. Carl Rogers holds that, just as a wounded limb will heal itself if the doctor provides the right conditions, so there are curative forces within the psyche which will start to function creatively once the emotional blocks which have hindered wholesome development are removed. The objective of the client-centred therapist therefore is not to advise or persuade the client to think or do anything for which he is not ready, still less to 'make him over' so that he is adjusted to the normal culture pattern of his society; it is dispassionately to reflect his feelings and thereby enable him to clarify and integrate them for himself so that he may eventually find his own core of selfhood and function from that.

Among artists, the words from Browning's *Paracelsus* illustrate a poet's insight into the same truth:

> 'And to know
> Rather consists in opening out a way
> Whence the imprisoned splendour can escape,
> Than in imposing entry for a light
> Supposed to be without.'

And, finally, among philosophers this same tentative spirit of enquiry into truth can be illustrated from Plato, of whom Gilbert Murray tells us 'It is characteristic of Greek thought that Plato never dogmatises, but always approaches truth by a dialogue, an argument between different points of view, and almost always leaves at the end some doubt, some feeling that although we have got deeper we have not quite reached the complete truth.'

This non-dogmatic, exploring, impersonal and unprejudiced approach to truth, with its faith in God immanent in man, and its corresponding educational practice of helping truth to unfold from within, instead of trying to impose it from without, is in harmony with the teaching of all great religions as to the way in which spiritual meanings can be revealed to spiritual understanding.

The phrase used by Jesus to describe this kind of understanding, this power of creative insight in man, was 'the kingdom of heaven'. He had the greatest difficulty in convincing his hearers, not only those who like the wife of Zebedee wanted preferential treatment for their families in this Kingdom, but even His own disciples, that he was talking about an inner condition, not a material one.

He would have the same difficulty in enabling people today to grasp this concept (and indeed some literalists would challenge His terminology, since they feel kingdoms are very out of date and Heaven should at least be a republic).

'My Kingdom is not of this world' makes sense when you can picture another and better place in the skies; but 'the Kingdom of Heaven is within you' seems a meaningless remark to many people, and Jehovah's Witnesses therefore explain that it really means 'the Kingdom is nigh'. Instead of trying to understand it, they prefer to wait for 'the coming of the Kingdom' from outside; an external and cataclysmic event which will automatically solve all life's problems.

Jesus tried in parable after parable to convey the meaning of the Kingdom, searching out the most significant symbols and stories He could find. When asked by the disciples, 'Who is the greatest in the Kingdom of Heaven?' He gave the surprising answer: 'Whosoever shall humble himself as this little child, the same is the greatest in the kingdom of heaven.' The parables of the Labourers, the Marriage of the King's Son, the Vineyard, the Fig Tree, the Wise and Foolish Virgins and the Talents all give explicit teaching on the nature of the Kingdom and the kind of people qualified to enter it. Perhaps the most illuminating parables are those concerned with growth. The parable of the Sower, 'The good seed are the children of the Kingdom', and two short parables in Mark, 'The Kingdom of God is as if a man should scatter seed upon the ground . . . and the seed should sprout and grow, he knows not how. The earth produces of itself, first the blade, then the ear, then the full grain in the ear.' Then He finds one image which vividly expresses the immense growth potential in small and almost invisible beginnings, the tremendous reach and power in the life of the spirit. 'With what can we compare the kingdom of God, or what parable shall we use for it? It is like a grain of mustard seed, which, when sown upon the ground, is the smallest of all the seeds on earth; yet when it is sown, it grows up and becomes the greatest of all shrubs, and puts forth large branches, so that the birds of the air can make nests in its shade'. And again: 'It is like leaven which a woman took and hid in three measures of meal, till it was all leavened' (Luke xiii. 20).

These three parables illustrate the stupendous power and potentiality in the abundant life of the spirit, once the seed has been planted and taken root in good soil. The two following illustrate its paramountcy: 'The kingdom of heaven is like treasure hidden in a field, which a man found and covered up; then in his joy he goes and sells all that he has and buys that field.' Again, the kingdom of heaven is like a merchant in search of fine pearls, who, on finding one pearl of great value, went and sold all that he had and bought it' (Matt. xiii. 44, 45). In other words, when the meaning of the Kingdom has been clearly understood, everything else becomes secondary.

The so-called great religions of the world are great not because of their size and the complexity of their systems, but because, and in so far as, they show insight into this same truth—a truth which can only be apprehended by those who have, in however small a degree, some experience of it.

Zen Buddhism, for example, teaches that the only knowledge that has any value and significance for us is that which we discover for ourselves. We must extract the meaning of life's experiences as they flow, and not expect any easy short-cuts to truth. The business of teachers and preachers should not be to tell, but to arouse us to the quest. The authoritarian way of telling all the answers may seem more time- and trouble-saving, but in the long run it will be seen to be valueless because no truth is ours that is not personally worked for and inwardly experienced. Moreover, there is always the danger that we shall start to care more for the authority than for the truth, for the Teacher than for the Way.

There is also the teaching of the Tao in Chinese thought; 'Tao' being the name for the Way, or Light, or Seed of God within the soul:

'If one look for Tao, there is nothing solid to see:
If one listens for it, there is nothing loud enough to hear.
Yet if one uses it, it is inexhaustible.'

And again:

'Tao is hidden and nameless,
Yet Tao alone supports all things and brings them to fulfilment.'[10]

The brief and cogent Veda '*Tat tvam asi*' ('Thou art That') is saying the same thing. So was St. Paul in the words: 'Your bodies are the Temple of the Holy Spirit.' Jesus said it was expedient for Him to go away in order that we might be open to receive this Spirit and not remain in dependence on Him personally, for it was this new birth and life of the Spirit that He said he had come to bring. A Christian mystic of our own day has written of this Life: 'The Religion of the Spirit does not depend for its power upon organisation. It does not pride itself upon any external claims. It talks little of infallibilities. It begins in the human soul like a tiny grain of mustard seed, but it expands like swiftly growing yeast and it works from individual to individual like invisible molecular forces . . . stealing in through the crannies of the world like so many soft rootlets, or like the capillary oozing of water, yet rending the hardest moments of man's pride if you give them time'. . . . It, too, has authority, but it is a different kind of authority. It is like the authority which beauty has over the rapt beholder, or that truth has over the mind convicted by it. . . . It rests its hope and faith entirely upon the irresistible might of the living Spirit of God revealing Himself in man's soul and working triumphantly forward by the contagion of truth and goodness.'[11] Where this spirit exists religion has achieved maturity, and there is no place for authoritarianism.

CHAPTER XII

FROM THE AUTHORITARIAN
APPROACH TO THE INWARD:
III. IN MORALITY

The patient is sick because he has neglected his soul's demands.

ERIC FROMM: *Psychoanalysis and Religion.*

The choice is always ours. Then, let me choose
The longest art, the hard Promethean way
Cherishingly to tend and feed and fan
That inward fire, whose small precarious flame,
Kindled or quenched, creates
The noble or the ignoble men we are,
The worlds we live in and the very fates,
Our bright or muddy star.[1]

ALDOUS HUXLEY.

WE HAVE SEEN THAT in the sphere of education author-itarian domination is beginning to give place to a scientific study of the child. In bygone days, when the master taught John Latin, the emphasis was on the Latin; to-day it is on John. Not only has the child become more important than the subject, but we have discovered that the Latin will be much more effectively learnt if John feels an interest in it, or at least a worthwhile motive for learning it. Even more important, we have discovered that some children cannot learn unless they have a friendly relationship to the person who is trying to teach them. In short, the sanction for teach-ing John Latin or anything else lies, not in the arbitrary opinions of authority, but in an objective study of the nature

191

of John and of his interests and capacities in relation to the opportunities and requirements of the world he will eventually have to enter.

Has there been any corresponding revolution in the sphere of ethics and of morality? Yes; here too the science of human nature is pointing the way to a new sanction for morality in the nature of man himself. In the past, the individual has been able to find out what was right by reference to the authority above him—parents, Church, State, etc. The sanction for doing it lay in the punishment those authorities had power to inflict. To-day, in democratic countries, that power is considerably diminished, and thoughtful people of all ages want to find out for themselves what is right by personal and unbiased exploration

But finding is one thing and doing is another. Children have been known to show very good sense in making their own school rules, and then to fail to keep them. Adults also have discovered good reasons for keeping the Commandments, independently of Church authority, in that the welfare of society as a whole requires it. But the questions then arise: Why should I worry about the welfare of society? What has society done for me? As the philosopher Hume somewhat brutally expressed it, 'Is there any reason why I should not prefer the death of a hundred people to the pricking of my own little finger?' The new 'moral scientists', the psychotherapists, are tending to say: 'Yes; there is a reason, and it lies not outside us in the sphere of external punishment; it lies in what Herbert Spencer called 'the discipline of natural consequences'—not, however, the external consequences Spencer had in mind, but the internal consequences in the nature of man himself. All life is governed by law, and man is part of life. One of the most basic laws of his being is the law of love. Christ gave it as the only law, embracing all others. The man who breaks this law by indifference to, or hatred of, his fellow men will pay the penalty in his own nature. He will become unlovable, unloved, and finally ill in mind or body or both.

What then do the scientists of human nature report? What is the new sanction for morality that has been discovered? It is essentially the same that was revealed by Jesus when He healed the man sick of the palsy—namely, the close connection between health and virtue. The man in the story was really 'sick' of his sins. Love and forgiveness eased his mind and cured his body. Whether the cure was permanent would depend on whether he was able to keep his life henceforth in line with his values, and to abide in the new power which had been brought to him. His cure was made possible by the fact that he wanted to be made whole. Wanting is the first step; not to want wholeness is itself part, perhaps the major part, of a diseased mind. But wanting is not enough unless one is prepared to do something for oneself as well as to receive aid from another, to pay the price of spiritual health in the self-discipline necessary to integrity. not to leave the matter at praying, 'Make and keep me pure within', but to see to it that one has done all in one's power to achieve such purity of motive, has come to grips with one's own nature and left nothing hidden from oneself.

> 'My strength is as the strength of ten
> Because my heart is pure.'

Sir Galahad's statement sounds a little priggish to modern ears, but his diagnosis was psychologically sound. In a 'pure' heart, no energy is wasted in holding back part of the price. Therefore life's forces can flow together harmoniously instead of in conscious or unconscious antagonism to each other.

The mentally sick who go to an analyst on the assumption that they can be cured by some hidden mysteries known only to the doctor, that the latter has up his sleeve the mental equivalent of insulin or cortisone, are doomed to disappointment. Jung gives an interesting example of this kind of mistake. He cites the case of a very intelligent young man who went through a long process of reductive analysis and could not understand why his symptoms did not disappear at the end of it, as rationally speaking, he felt they should have done. Then, almost by chance, Jung discovered that the answer lay, not where they had been looking, but in the fact that the young man's attitude to life was somehow fundamentally wrong. . . . 'His want of conscience was the cause of his neurosis. He had supposed that by invoking scientific thought, he could spirit away the immorality which he himself could not stomach.'[2] That is to say, his deeper self could not stomach it, and so produced the symptoms. His surface self wanted to be cured of these symptoms, but without paying the price in change of attitude; and, indeed, he was unwilling to admit that any such change was needed, since the friend he was exploiting 'did not mind'. The symptoms therefore remained, because the law of our being requires integrity, and psychiatry has no magic by which that law can be evaded.

Fromm gives a similar example of a patient suffering from spells of dizziness caused by the fact that he was finding excuses for acting against his own convictions. But his 'basic moral personality' would not let him get by with this and produced a symptom which forced him to face up to his own inner conflict. He recovered his health when he recovered his integrity.

(It should not be deduced from such cases that all illness is caused, in the last resort, by lack of inner integrity. The recent stress on psychosomatic illness is a valuable corrective to the previous refusal to look at anything but physical causes; but in some people it has become an over-reaction, and they attempt to explain all illness in strictly psychological terms. It is therefore necessary to remind the one-track mind that bad diet or some other physical factor *may* be the cause of stomach ulcers, that rickets may be due to lack of calcium rather than to lack of conscience, and scurvy to insufficient vitamin C rather than to inner moral conflict.

It should also be noted that breaking the moral law does

not necessarily produce neurotic symptoms unless there is a state of unconscious conflict. Furthermore, it is possible that a symptom may be 'cured' without a fundamental change of character. A symptom may disappear from one area of operation to reappear in different form in another if the cause of the illness is not reached, e.g. claustrophobia may give place to stammering or nail-biting to 'nerves'.)

In the two above cases it was the breaking of the law of integrity which caused ill health; sometimes it is the breaking of the law of growth, the failure to go forward. On the psychological plane there is no mother bird to eject us forcibly from the nest when it is time to learn to fly. Consequently, many people who are adult in years and intellect are still infantile in their emotions. They were unable or unwilling to face the difficulties involved in growing up, and so, finding excuses for clinging to the condition of protected dependency, they drift gradually and inevitably towards 'The Wilderness of the Lost'. This type of neurotic, designated by Anton Boisen 'the drifter', may seem for a time to be harmless and amiable enough. He may even develop a high degree of ability in some sphere of occupation that appeals to him; but he will accept no discipline and make no effort unless he feels like it. In the early stages of neurosis he is not 'bad' in any positive sense, and indeed may seem singularly free from aggression and hate. But his distaste for effort makes him eventually incapable of anything save easy modes of satisfaction, and if these are denied he begins to show anger and violence, and to take refuge from the cruel world in a resort to drink or drugs. Far from choosing 'the hard Promethean Way', he has chosen the way of immediate satisfactions on the instinctual level, and, since we must always be getting either better or worse, a stage comes when he can no longer make good even if he wanted, and he drifts ever further 'down to dissolution and destruction. As disintegration continues, malignant character tendencies increase'[3] and the 'Descent into Hell' becomes inevitable.

Such a marked degree of immaturity is fortunately not

common, but we are all failing in our degree to live in accordance with the moral and spiritual laws to which we do lip service, partly from weakness of will, partly because we have found no religion sufficiently convincing to require us to live continuously in accordance with those laws.

It is clear to those who have had any close contact with neurotics that, however little they may be responsible for the origin of their neuroses in infancy, their problems are basically moral, and that the ill-health from which they suffer is often hypochondriacal in nature, an expression of their infantile self-concern and of their failure to meet life's demands with courage. Jung's over-intellectualised patient insisted that 'morals have nothing to do with science'. He was sure a good doctor would be able to cure his symptom without reference to his morals. But he remained sick, and Jung came to the conclusion (a conclusion that will doubtless cause the religious to smile) that it is a grave error for the psychologist to ignore the moral factor in therapy.

Yet the religious can also be grateful for the psychological support which brings a scientific basis to his teaching. The difference is that 'humanistic ethics' finds the sanction for good behaviour in the nature of man himself, not in authority of Church or Scripture. It says that the things we disapprove: selfishness, laziness, hypocrisy, escapism, greed, self-pity and the rest—all these are bad, not because of the Ten Commandments or any other authoritarian legislation, but because they are *bad for us*; they don't work, and sooner or later they make us ill. Scientific study of man's nature and mental illnesses shows that if he tries to be opportunist and make the best of both worlds, serving God and Mammon simultaneously, to that extent he will be schizoid or two-centred. If he shirks the inevitable growing pains of development, he will end up with very much worse pains in the long run. So not only honesty, but all virtuous behaviour is in fact 'the best policy'; though if we follow it solely for that reason, we may be moral, but we shall not be virtuous.

There is nothing new in all this: it is only the scientific

approach to it that is new. Great minds throughout the ages from Buddha to Gandhi, from Protagoras to Whitehead, have known that Socrates spoke truly when he said that 'To desert the path of life according to principle is the ultimate stupidity'. Spinoza declared that 'Avarice, ambition, lust, etc., are a kind of madness, although they are not reckoned among diseases'. They are indeed 'a kind of madness' because they hinder the way of man's creative advance, and will eventually cause sickness to his soul and perhaps to his body.

But, it may be objected at this point, the term 'morality' is equivocal. People have differing ideas about right and wrong; there are also varying 'patterns of culture' and one tribe or nation may disapprove the standards of another. The Moslems, for example, believe that laws should be made at the level of average need, and hence four wives are regarded as a reasonable compromise with man's nature.

That is true, but in this discussion we are concerned with the subjective approach to the matter, with spiritual wholeness, not with objective right. A man must do what he believes to be right even if subsequent events prove that he was objectively wrong. We may make mistakes of judgement and still be functioning from our true centre; still be integrated. The philosopher Kant said: 'When the "Thou shalt" of the moral law, becomes the "I will" of the soul, then we are free.' He might have added, 'And then we are whole', because the conscious will is now in accord with the value judgements of the self.

What did Kant mean by the moral law? Did he mean a legal code like the codes of Hammurabbi, Solon, or Napoleon? Obviously not, for there is nothing in these to fill the mind with that awe and wonder which Kant claimed he experienced whenever he contemplated the starry heavens above or the moral law within. No; he meant what Socrates meant when he spoke of the 'sign of God' within, the prophetic sign on which he relied for guidance; what the Psalmist meant when he affirmed 'Thy law is within my heart'; what Buddha meant by the *Dharma* or Right Path; what Lao-tzu meant by the *Tao*; and what Jesus meant by the Way.

Civil laws like those of Leviticus and Numbers are necessary expedients for the smooth running of the society for which they have been devised. But they do not 'rejoice the heart and give light unto the eyes; nor are they to be described as 'sweeter than honey and the honeycomb' or to evoke the exclamation, 'How I do love Thy law!' It is clear, therefore, that Kant and the rest were referring to something else: they were referring to the spiritual law that is inherent in the nature of things, the law of love, courage, growth and integrity. They were also referring to that part of man's being which is responsive to spiritual law, the part of him which has been variously described as the moral consciousness, the inner Light, the divine immanence, the soul, etc., the part of him that knows that 'right action is treasured in the nature of things',[4] but does not necessarily tell him in detail what is right, since his growth depends on finding that out for himself; which tells him he must ever go forward toward fuller life, but does not provide him with an ordnance map; which makes him love righteousness and hate iniquity without always being sure which is which. To give explicit direction for each step would be to deprive man of the chief characteristics of his humanity his power of choice, and his capacity for development.

For this reason, any democratic group, home, school or nation will be flexible and allow wide differences of opinion so long as they do not endanger the security of the whole. They will understand that the truth is hard to come by and that throughout the ages equally good and sincere men have been known to hold opposing views on the best way to implement an agreed principle. St. Peter, like Socrates,[5] urged that 'We ought to obey God rather than men'. We ought, that is, to do what we in all sincerity believe to be right, even if we are in fact mistaken.

'The price of freedom is eternal vigilance'; the price is

also some degree of confusion, and some suffering, resulting from the harm that even good men do. But however much confusion and misunderstanding is involved, it is better to be mistaken and 'fooled' than to be repressive or suspicious; better to tolerate a 'Red Dean' than to have a barren uniformity of opinion based on fear; better to find a place for the conscientious objector, whether to war or to vaccination, than force people to violate their own intuition of the will of God.

The immature and dependent mind that has been in the habit of turning to some external authority for direction in the sphere of values may ask, when told that the only authority lies within himself, 'Then does it matter very much what I do if it's all subjective, and if there is no punishment in the hereafter for wrongdoing?' It does matter; and the reason lies in the nature of man. Man is part of creation and law is operative throughout all creation. Therefore every conscious creature must find and follow the law of its being, must fulfil its own entelechy. The entelechy of an acorn is to become an oak, of a caterpillar to become a butterfly, and so on. Man's entelechy is different from that of plant or animal, infinitely more complex, and with infinitely greater possibilities for good and evil. To fulfil his destiny as a human being, man must grow away from the 'pre-genital' stage, from that which is greedy, dependent, fear-full, infantile, towards that which is productive, creative and mature and differentiated. He must because he can, and because this is the 'natural' trend of his development. But though natural, it is not easy or inevitable; he has the choice. If he shrinks from it, clings to earlier levels, nurses attitudes of self-pity and self-indulgence, then sooner or later life steps in, and through the medium of mental and/or physical illness, warns him that something is wrong with the growth process that the laws of his humanity are being broken and that he needs awakening to the fact. Hence an attack of 'nerves', insomnia, or any other psycho-physical illness *may* be a blessing in disguise. But because he is a free

199

being he need not take the warning; he may decide on the way of escapism and retreat from the moral struggle, and risk the consequences. If he believes that in this life only we have hope, there is, of course, good sense, from the materialist point of view, in making the 'most' of this life and being self-indulgent and merry or miserable while it lasts, especially if the deluge is going to be let loose on us at any moment. But if the soul has reality, then not only must we say that materialism is folly, but that righteousness must be loved for itself and virtuous action must be followed not from fear of consequence, but because the good is seen as the beautiful, as the Greeks saw it when they coined the one word *kalagathos*, the beautiful-good.

And while obeying the moral law of the land is a social necessity and therefore wise and prudent, love of virtue for its own sake will bring good health to the soul and an accompanying inner power as known to Jesus when he said: 'Virtue has gone out of Me.' Therefore wrote Milton:

> Love vertue, she alone is free,
> She can teach ye how to clime
> Higher than the Spheary chime;
> Or if Vertue feeble were,
> Heav'n itself would stoop to her.

CHAPTER XIII

FROM THE PROVINCIAL APPROACH
TO THE UNIVERSAL: I. RELIGIONS

Whosoever comes to Me, through whatsoever form, I reach him.
All men are struggling through paths which in the end lead
to Me.

Bhagavad Gita.

To those who keep their eyes on the 'one thing needful' denom-
inations, creeds, ceremonies, the conclusions of philosophy . . .
are matters of comparative indifference. They represent merely
the different angles from which the soul may approach that simple
union with Brahma which is its goal; and are useful only in so
far as they contribute to this consummation.

EVELYN UNDERHILL: Introduction to *Songs of Kabir.*

'AND WHAT ARE THE chances that Japan will now become
a Christian country'? asked an American evangelist of a
visitor returning from the Far East. 'I am afraid there is no
likelihood of that,' was the reply. 'It seems to me certain
that they will keep their own religions of Buddhism and
Shintoism.' The evangelist was silent for a moment and then
commented: 'That is very sad news for us Christians.'

James Michener, a contemporary student of the Far
East, also has no encouragement for the missionaries. He
writes: 'I happen to believe strongly in the Christian faith . . .
but I suspect that in the long run it may well be some

Oriental religion infinitely older than Christianity that will provide the spiritual leadership for that part of the world. No one can overlook the fact that Asians happen to be totally committed to their religions which in certain respects serve them even better than Christianity serves us. . . . What is likely is that each of the great religions of Asia will retain authority in its allotted geographic area and that in each religion the many good points will triumph over the obvious weaknesses.'[1]

The really regrettable thing is not that the people of the East should want to retain their own form of religious expression; it is that the Western evangelist should regard that natural fact as regrettable; should assume that no religion can have any validity save his own; and should fail to realise that it is easy enough to change the name of one's gods or the form of one's ritual without any corresponding inner change.

The opposite viewpoint is maintained in this book—namely, that religion is a wider and deeper concept than belief in any particular creed—indeed, that it is possible to be a deeply religious person without subscribing to a religious creed; just as it is also possible to be an irreligious 'believer'—to lay hold of the form and miss the meaning: and, moreover, that it is possible for mature Christians, or Hindus, Moslems or others, to retain their allegiance to their own religion, and yet agree with each other on the underlying truth which is common to all and which unites all more strongly and fundamentally than superficial differences divide.

People with this outlook who seek for the Highest Common Factor to all religions, instead of trying to make one dominate the rest, build the foundation for real religious unity, as distinct from uniformity. There is no safe place left in this closely welded world for the egocentricity of provincialism, either in religion, politics, nationalism or anything else.

But this does not mean that local religions should be

discarded; it means only that a different attitude should be cultivated towards them. It means seeing them as different varieties of vessel holding the same treasure; different roads to the same goal; different children of the same family, or whatever other analogy one may find to express unity in diversity. One road to truth may be, in some respects, superior to another, in which case let the fact be noted. But if our eyes are on the goal we shall not quarrel about the approach to it, still less try to impose our own particular approach on others.

It is therefore surprising to find a philosopher like Santayana deprecating recent attempts to formulate a synthesis of the world's great historic religions, and implying that such a synthesis would abolish all diversity of form and expression, for it does not imply any such thing. In one of his last conversations, Santayana is reported as saying: 'Religion is always local and mythical—despite what people like Aldous Huxley may say—and it is *morally true*. . . . It is impossible to define in words. I prefer to be frankly poetical and say I am content to rest on the bosom of Abraham.'[2]

The contradiction expressed here is false. There is no necessary antithesis between the local and poetic expressions of religion, and the highest common factor that unites them all. Neither Aldous Huxley in *Perennial Philosophy* nor Gerald Heard in *The Eternal Gospel* is concerned to criticise or abolish the local and poetic; only to demonstrate the uniting thread, the common ground that has been the root source of inspiration to all religions throughout the ages. Being able to trace this Common Ground, this Perennial Philosophy, does not necessitate discarding the local and poetic expression of it. Those who find imagery helpful should continue to use it, always seeking to rely more on the meaning and less on the image, and always remembering the warning of Eckhart that 'He who seeks God under settled form lays hold of the form while missing the God concealed in it'.

Much of the provincialism and deplorable proselytising in the Christian religion is due to the failure to distinguish between form and content, between the literal and the poetic, between verbal statement and significant meaning. One result of this literalness is the unfortunate habit some people have of lifting a text from the Bible, disregarding its context, and then interpreting it in accordance with their own conscious or unconscious desires. Such a text for example as 'Go ye into all the world and preach the gospel to every creature' is readily used as an excuse for sallying forth to convert the 'unenlightened', especially by the youthful enthusiast in need of a crusading outlet for his ego. A careful and analytic study of what Jesus meant by 'the gospel', of His insistence on the inwardness of the Kingdom, might forestall such crude salvationalism. The internal evidence of the New Testament portrays Him as placing much emphasis on courageous and independent thinking; on meditating deeply on the spirit rather than on the letter of the law; on intuitive understanding and loving service of one's fellows, even when it clashes with authoritarian dictates: but no emphasis whatsoever on doctrine and correct belief. In the parable of the Last Judgement, the 'saved' are not the orthodox, but the humanitarian.

Man's mind is such that he has always found it easier to cling to certain 'concrete' beliefs *about* his great leaders than to enter into the spirit of their teaching. We like a theology that is tidy, specific, clearly stated and capable of being clearly envisaged. As Rilke puts it:

> 'All those who find Thee bind Thee
> To gesture and to form.'[3]

Things must be black or white, right or wrong; no 'dusty answers'. 'Spirit' is too vague a thing to visualise and fill with content; 'grow and develop' is a more difficult and indefinite directive than 'believe and be saved'.

Another reason why people retain a fundamentalist

attitude is their subconscious fear that the serious and impartial study of other scriptures might reveal truths which then could not be ignored, and which would necessitate an entire re-evaluation of their position. This might result in a loss of faith and emotional insecurity too alarming to contemplate, and would probably be accompanied by a sense of guilt over the 'disloyalty' to one's own Church and creed.

But such a fear of loss and such a sense of guilt are the product of a narrow and mistaken religious education, based on ignorance of our own psychology. Alfred Adler claimed that the strongest motivation in our make-up is the drive towards superiority; the 'positive self-feeling' that likes not only to be in the right, but to be in the position to tell others what is right without contradiction. Whether or not Alder was correct in claiming that this is our strongest drive, it is unquestionably very strong as anyone who looks carefully and honestly at himself must agree. The longing to feel superior is not, of course, peculiar to religion, any more than the concept of 'God's Chosen People' was peculiar to the Jews. It pervades every department of life, social, industrial, political, and all others. But religion offers a very special kind of alibi under which, in the name of piety, the feeling of superiority can take cover. For example, the still popular Christian hymn asks with touching candour:

> 'Shall we whose souls are lighted
> With wisdom from on high,
> Shall we to men benighted
> The lamp of life deny?'

This hymn suggests that it is our duty and destiny, rather than our desire, to impose the truth on others. How the people of Ceylon, whose culture and civilisation go back over two thousand, five hundred years, like being referred to as 'benighted', or at hearing that every prospect pleases on

205

their lovely island save its 'vile' inhabitants, are questions needing no answer.

Another popular hymn grieves that—

> 'O'er heathen lands afar
> Thick darkness broodeth yet';

to which observation the 'heathen' in question might reasonably reply, 'Thank you very much, but please leave us in our darkness; for if being enlightened means the ability to think up such things as atom bombing, we think darkness is preferable.' The Jews and Turks also might be pardoned for feeling some resentment when the English Church prays for them on Good Friday that, along with other infidels and heretics, they may be delivered from 'all ignorance and hardness of heart and contempt of Thy word'. It seems to have been overlooked that the Jews gave us our Scriptures, for which gift it would be more polite to say a word of thanks than of criticism. To the arrogance of the thoughtless evangelist (no less harmful for being unconscious), the Indian philosopher makes this simple reply: 'Your Christian civilisation is ending in disaster, and you are bold enough to offer it to others.'[4]

But proselytising is not confined to those of other creeds, and climes. The following pious expression of 'Christian' charity illustrates the terrifying strength of the drive towards superiority even within the fold of one religion: 'Roman Catholics have divine authority for burning all Protestants and sending them to the infernal flames.'[5] That being so, it is not surprising that one Roman Catholic priest in East Africa is reported to have described Protestants as '*Kuni ya Shatani*' ('the Devil's Firewood'), or that a Swahili geography book should inform its readers that 'The Protestants are the mischief-makers in religion who have perverted the truth of the Word. . . . These mischief-makers are chiefly found in England, Germany, Scandinavia, etc.'[6] But lest this should suggest that any one group has the prerogative in intolerance, or that Catholicism is always totalitarian, let it be noted than an ex-Jesuit priest, Leonard Feeney, was recently excommunicated by the Pope for preaching on Boston Common against Protestants and Jews, and for declaring that there is no salvation for non-Catholics. Let us also remind Protestants of the unjust legislation against Roman Catholics in nineteenth-century England which denied them many civic rights; or of the vandalism of people like the infamous Protestant Kensit brothers, who used to demonstrate their devotion to truth and Christian charity by smashing up the images in Anglo-Catholic churches and by creating a rowdy disturbance at the most sacred moment of the Eucharist. The fascist spirit can, and does, exist anywhere.

In contrast to such bigotry, it is refreshing to remember that there have been outstanding Christian missionaries, Catholic and Protestant, to whom missionary work was a matter of sharing rather than of converting; who set no value on counting heads, but who sought to learn as well as to teach, to understand as well as to be understood. In West Africa, Albert Schweitzer put so much emphasis on service and loving-kindness, and so little on dogma, that fellow Christians have been known to question his Christianity. In China, Richard Wilhelm found that he received so richly from those he had intended to teach that he was able to give to the world the priceless products of his studies of the ancient Chinese Yoga system, the description of 'the secret of the powers of growth latent in the psyche'. Among other names worthy of remembrance in this field are those of Carey, who won a sympathetic ear from the wise men of Bengal, and at the same time interested them in the Christian stress on brotherhood and social service; Pennell, who, unarmed and unafraid, lived his teaching of non-violence among the violent men of the North-West Frontier; and C. F. Andrews, friend of Tagore and Gandhi, who wrote to his fellow missionaries: 'It is no part of your call, I assure you, to tear up the lives of the people of the East by the roots.'

Let it not be thought that this emphasis on mutual respect and understanding carries the implication that any one religion is as good as any other. The religions of the world obviously embody an enormous range of mental and spiritual development. The range from such a 'religion' as Voodooism, which consists mainly of sorcery, to the Hinduism of a Ramakrishna is considerable. But not only is this true. There is also an enormous difference in the levels of understanding and in the quality of expression within any one religion; indeed, there is often greater unanimity between the liberal-minded of different creeds than between devotees of the same creed. There would obviously be greater kinship of spirit between Dean Inge and Rabindranath Tagore than between Dean Inge and Billy Sunday. Yet the two latter are both called 'Christians'. Under this one title also come the Holy Rollers and Cardinal Newman; Aimee Semple Mac-Pherson and St. Therese; Gipsy Smith and Baron von Hugel. For some, Christianity is little more than an emotional orgy which holds the intellect in contempt; for others it calls forth a high quality of restraint, scholarship and maturity of insight. Yet in spite of these great differences between relatively primitive and relatively mature religions, as well as between relatively primitive and mature people within any one religion, the fact remains that there is to all the great religions of the world a changeless Tradition, a Perennial Philosophy or Gospel of eternal value.

'Which has not taught weak wills how much they can?
Which has not fall'n on the dry heart like rain?
Which has not cried to sunk self-weary man:
        "Thou must be born again:" '

Via this Common Ground, men like Gandhi and Ramakrishna have found it possible to join the Christian Church for a time, and to take part in its worship and services without any idea of becoming official Christians. Ramakrishna practised Islamic disciplines for a period, and felt that all had validity and all led to the same goal, though for himself, he naturally preferred as do most men, the way to which he was attuned by birth, temperament and training.

Another illustration of this broad and deep approach is given us by the fifteenth-century poet Kabir: 'So thorough-going is Kabir's eclecticism that he seems by turns Vedan-tist and Vaishnavite, Brahman and Sufi, Pantheist and Transcendentalist. In the effort to tell the truth about that ineffable apprehension, so vast and yet so near, which con-stitutes his life, he seizes and twines together . . . symbols, and ideas drawn from the most violent and conflicting philosophies and faiths. All are needed if he is ever to suggest the character of that One whom the Upanishads call "the Sun-coloured being who is beyond this Darkness" as all the colours of the spectrum are needed if we would demon-strate the simple richness of white light. In thus adapting traditional materials to his own use, he follows a method common among the mystics, who seldom exhibit any special love for originality of form. They will pour their wine into almost any vessel that comes to hand; generally using by preference—and lifting to new levels of significance—the religious or philosophic formulae current in their own day.'[7]

In 1893, Vivekananda came from India to attend the Parliament of Religions in Chicago. He expressed surprise when some of his American followers asked, 'Shall we now leave our own Church?' Nothing was further from his mind. He pointed out that the search for common ground, for deeper underlying truth, did not necessitate the abandon-ment of one's own customary form of religious expression. On the contrary, variety of expression in this sphere can be as good and enriching a thing as it can among individuals, nations and races. Only when one group, without any real knowledge of other groups, insists that its own religious creed is not only the best, but the only true one, is trouble caused. The more imaginative spirit, capable of wider horizons, would agree with Zenephon that 'When God is our teacher, we come to think alike'—to think alike, that is, so far as the eternal verities are concerned. Were we all to think alike about all debatable details, we should soon not be thinking at all. It is through friendly interchange in an atmosphere of freedom and interest that new thought comes to birth, and new connections are seen; not by the imposition of a barren uniformity of outlook. We should no more be afraid of exposing our religion to contact and comparison with other religions than of exposing it to the scrutiny of science, for 'There is no way of preserving truth so effective as to give it an open field with error. When the breezes blow the chaff flies. When a barrier shuts off the wind from the grain, the wheat is never winnowed.'[8]

The best friends of religion are those who realise that true Christianity would be enriched and vitalised, not weakened, by studying the life of the Orient; since Buddhism, Judaism, Islam, Taoism, Confucianism, Shintoism all have something of great value to contribute to Christianity, just as Christianity has something of great value to contribute to them. For the ignorance is not one-sided; there are many Buddhists who know no more of Christianity than the average Christian knows of Buddhism. By sheltering themselves from each other, each is the loser; each becomes less interesting and less influential. The deeper meanings that might be opened up, the creative insights that might be fostered by friendly sharing and mutual interest in the common theme of religion remain unrealised,

It is therefore very encouraging to read of the movement recently inaugurated at Oxford by a group of distinguished men whose purpose is 'to promote the scientific and comparative study of religion in the interest of inter-religious understanding and international peace'. The new note to be welcomed here is the emphasis on the essentials of religion rather than on their exoteric formulation; the recognition that variety is possible without contradiction; and that a spirit of mutual appreciation and respect can and must replace the old attitude of superiority and exclusiveness.

This is a creative and unifying approach. It recognises that while the essential core of the religious tradition has been the same throughout the ages, different aspects of the Tradition are stressed by different peoples at different times. At the present time the stress of Christianity is on social betterment. The East is learning from the West in this respect, and we in our turn could learn much from the East as to the more inward and psychological approach. In this spirit of emphasising the complementary rather than the competitive, the comparative study of religions should be thought-provoking, not strife-provoking, and it would have immense value for, and bring great happiness to, those whose interest is in the religious life rather than in a religion. (The comparative study of religions carried on in this spirit appears to be less uncommon in America than in Europe. The University of Chicago and the University of Southern California are especially to be noted for scholarly work in this sphere.)

Such study would also deepen man's understanding of his fellows and thereby help to cement friendship in the family of nations. For what is true of mankind is also true of his religions. They are many, they are imperfect, but they too are not 'islands' complete in themselves. Below the surface, in intention and direction, they are one, their deep common purposes being the unitive knowledge of God. And if it is true that 'God hath not at any time left Himself without a witness', then it cannot also be true that He revealed himself to one people at one time only, and gave one formula for salvation to one Church alone. Such exclusive action would not be consonant with the spiritual law as we know it. It would savour more of authoritarianism than of the educational and democratic way of encouraging the search for truth through individual growth, experience and experiment; of imposed uniformity rather than of that unity in diversity that makes life interesting and fruitful; of autocratic interference rather than of freedom to make mistakes and find a way for oneself.

Christianity does not cease to be true in its real and inward sense when it has the courage and the humility to recognise the validity of other approaches to God. If we admit that 'all holy scriptures are written for our learning',⁹ we must include, not only the scriptures of the Jews, but the Koran, the Tao teaching, the *Vedas*, the *Upanishads*, the *Bhagavad Gita*, and all other inspired literature, whether included in the canon or not.

An ancient Vedic hymn says with deep wisdom: 'As different streams having their sources in different places mingle their waters in the sea, so, O lord, the different paths men take through different tendencies, various though they appear, crooked or straight, all lead to Thee.' A modern Indian expresses the same truth: 'There are many paths that lead to the summit of one and the same mountains; their differences will be more apparent the lower down we are, but they vanish at the peak; each will naturally take the one that starts from the point at which he finds himself; he who goes round about the mountain looking for another is not climbing. Never let us approach another believer to ask him to become "one of us", but approach him with respect as one who is already one of His, who is, and from whose invariable beauty all contingent being depends.'¹⁰

Such a viewpoint will be anathema to those who do not wish to study any religion save their own, and to the literal-minded who feel that Christianity consists in believing the Bible, or at least the New Testament, 'from cover to cover,' without making any attempt at interpretation at a deeper level. Yet just such a reorientation in our thinking is necessary if we are to take that final step in religious tolerance which will make it possible for our Churches to become 'bridges across which all honest men may tread into the wider fellowship of mankind', and so set an example of toleration and humility in other spheres of life.

'God, being one, yet hath many names':

'May He who is the Father in Heaven of the Christians,
Allah of the Mohammedans,
Jehovah of the Jews,
Ahura Mazda of the Zoriastrians,
Buddha of the Buddhists,
Divine Mother Infinite and All-abiding Spirit of the
    Indu-Ayrans,
Grant unto all peace and blessing.'

CHAPTER XIV

FROM THE PROVINCIAL APPROACH
TO THE UNIVERSAL: II. RELIGION

Religion . . . is the vision of something which stands within,
behind and beyond the passing flux of immediate things; something which is real yet waiting to be realised; something which is
a remote possibility yet the greatest of all present facts; something
which gives meaning to all that passes, and yet, eludes apprehension; something whose possession is the final good and yet is
beyond all reach; something which is the ultimate ideal, the
hopeless quest. It gives to suffering its swift insight into the values
that can issue from it; it transmutes what has been lost into a
living fact within one's own nature; it is the mirror which
discloses to every creature his own greatness.

PROFESSOR A. N. WHITEHEAD.

WHAT, THEN, OF RELIGION, of that which 'lights the
altar of every creed' but is to be identified with none, of
that which is the core, the highest common factor of all
religions? What is its essential significance, as distinct from
any particular creed? Is there in fact any reality to this
concept that cannot be explained away in other terms?

'Nobody knows' was the answer recently given to this
question by one psychologist. He was, however, being quite
unnecessarily negative, for throughout the ages men and
women have given accounts of an experience which no
impartial investigator can regard as other than valid.
Granted that much that passes under the name of religion is
false: perhaps the projection of an emotional need for con-
solation or for power; perhaps a cover for political activities

or social advancement; these facts should not be allowed to blur or blot out the authenticity of the real thing.

It has been said that all human beings think better of humanity because Shakespeare and Beethoven had the power of saying more than mortal things. Our obligation as students of religion is to explore those 'more than mortal things', to see whether it is possible not merely to know *about* them, but to become attuned so that we can experience them for ourselves and thence distinguish between the authentic and the pseudo, between the words of eternal life and those of emotional escapism or disguised passion. No one who has not explored this path is in a position to pass judgement, for he will not know whereof he speaks.

Definitions of religion are numerous, but the majority make the same reference as Whitehead to 'something beyond'; to a realm of being commonly referred to as the supernatural.

The word 'supernatural' is misleading, because it suggests not only a different but an unnatural order of being. Perhaps it would be more helpful therefore to think in terms of our human limitations, to accept the proposition that there is 'only one universe', but that we, with our earth bodies, are 'obstructed' from apprehending more than a very little of it, and from discerning more than a very few of the relationships that unite the whole.

At our rudimentary stage of development, it would be an absurd presumption to claim exact or detailed knowledge of the transcendental. How can we possibly know save 'through a glass darkly'? Yet it would be equally foolish to ignore those intimations that we do receive of 'other dimensions'; or those intuitions which tell us that the life we know through the senses only has meaning and significance in relation to a larger life. The intuition may be dim and fleeting or it may be of such overwhelming wonder and beauty that the whole of life is changed by it. Both degrees of intensity are referred to by Francis Thompson in *The Hound of Heaven:*

'I dimly guess what time in mists confounds;
Yet ever and anon a trumpet sounds
From the hid battlements of Eternity.
Those shaken mists a space unsettle, then
Round the half-glimpsed turrets slowly wash again.'[1]

Another poet has described the unifying effect of that experience:

''Tis from thy centre to thine utmost bound
To feel that thou hast found—
That thou too art
From all to all eternity a part
Of that which never was in speech expressed,
The unresting order which is more than rest.'[2]

Such experience is referred to in various terms such as cosmic consciousness or the oceanic feeling, or the sense of the almost, or unitive knowledge of God. Always it is felt there is no longer any division between the here and the hereafter, the creature and the Creator, the self and the Self.

To the rationalist, such language is completely meaningless. What is more, he feels that if the mystic knows something, he should be able to describe it in clear terminology. What sense can the scientific mind make of such paradoxical lines as these:

'O world invisible, we view thee,
O world intangible, we touch thee,
O world unknowable, we know thee,
Inapprehensible, we clutch thee!'[3]

Since it is patently impossible to know the unknowable or to see the invisible, such words are therefore dismissed as meaningless rubbish; or at best as a charming phantasy. And yet to the mystic or the mystically inclined, they are the expression of profound insight into the nature of the unknown and of our relationship to it.

The language of mysticism is no more satisfactory to the average individual than it is to the rationalist, and so the majority of religions, with the exception of Taoism and Zen Buddhism, go a good deal further in attempting to say something explicit about this Reality which lies outside normal sensory experience. The abstract thinker may refer to It in non-personal terminology by such names as the Ground, the Source, the Inner Light, the Absolute, Brahman, the Tao or Way. But the majority of people, feeling It to be in some sense personal, prefer to use personal terms such as God, the All-Father, Allah, Jehovah, the Great Spirit, the Paraclete, the Mother, Shiva, and so on. The 'thousand and one' names are all inadequate, since 'no man hath seen God at any time'. They are also misleading because they give rise to images which tend to be taken for the Reality.

The rationalist dismisses these names with their corresponding images as even more nonsensical than the mystic's paradoxes, and he points to the exclusive and proselytising attitudes which the names help to encourage. But as the majority of men think with the aid of images, the names are useful so long as they are recognised for what they are: symbols, or vehicles of meaning; ways of referring to that Reality which 'no words can paint', but not to be identified with the Reality itself.

But what proof have we that there is any such Reality corresponding either to the names or to the mystic experience? And what proof have we that there is any essential difference between the ecstasy of the mystic and other forms of induced ecstasy, such as that of the drug addict?[4] No proof whatever of the type required, any more than one could prove the beauty of the sunset to a man who was colour-blind. Inner experiences are not capable of mathematical or logical formulation.

One thing we can say, however. Whatever similarity may exist between the psycho-physical condition of the addict and that of the mystic in the experience itself, there is none in the effects of the experience. One rapidly degenerates into a compulsion to which the individual becomes ever more enslaved until he finally loses grip on life and on himself; the other stimulates the individual to greater effort and self-ascendency in the furtherance of spiritual knowledge and achievement. The enslaved addict is at the mercy of his craving; and loses all power of will and choice; the mystic feels empowered to transcend his passions, and realises that the first law of spiritual alchemy requires that the Green Lion, the natural man, must be tamed before he can be given wings.

This distinction brings us to the second aspect of the religious life, the conative, active, striving aspect. Religion is not simply an experience; it is a way of life; it involves work, not passivity; and primarily work on ourselves, work towards increase of self knowledge and self-control. Here we tread on delicate ground because of the bad Puritan heritage which has stressed discipline and self-control for their own sakes, which has despised the body and turned sensory satisfaction into 'sin'; which has forgotten how to rejoice in the good things of life and has forbidden others to do so, bidding them instead to wallow in a sense of guilt with self-loathing for their sins—sins, like virtues, being thought of as so many isolated beads on a string, so many unrelated wrong acts.

In truth, sin is a serious matter, but it is an attitude rather than an act; for an act might be right for one and wrong for another. In general terms, sin might be defined as the failure to follow our own inner Light, as that way of thought or feeling that hinders our development, darkens our capacity for true insight, muddies our power of discrimination, and prevents us from going forward to fuller and happier awareness. Every mature individual must judge for himself whether a particular line of action would have this effect and would therefore be 'sinful' for him. The emphasis should be on the Path and on progress in it; and since certain things such as greed, hatred, fear, jealousy and vindictiveness, can obstruct that progress, we have to work at becoming freed from them if our intention is to follow the Path. All this is plain common sense, and has only become uncommon among certain groups who are in reaction against the bad puritanical legacy which concentrated on the negative, made renunciation an end in itself, saw evil in things that are not evil, and presented life as a thing to be endured rather than enjoyed.

It is not surprising that, as soon as they became free to do so, many people threw off this harsh picture of life and all its associated language and concepts, such as renunciation, mortification, purgation, discipline, training, and even self-control. Because of the grim and joyless asceticism that they evoke, it is better therefore to avoid them and replace them with more positive ones, such as discrimination, temperateness, integrity, wisdom, self-knowledge, detachment, etc. All these imply the necessity of some degree of discipline and control, but they keep the emphasis where it rightly belongs—on growth and advance towards a fuller life and enlightenment.

Going to extremes, oscillating back and forth from one absolute to another, is a common human weakness, and when religion is not being attacked from one side as escapism, self-indulgence, the 'opium of the people', it is being attacked from the other as asceticism and the deliberate cultivation of pain. There is, of course, plenty of justification for both attacks, for plenty of 'religious' people have been guilty of one or other excess. But religion itself is not guilty, for it advocates neither the one nor the other. What it advocates is athleticism not asceticism—that sane and necessary discipline which is accepted as unavoidable in the case of the athlete or the artist. Nobody challenges the former for strenuous practice in the gymnasium, or the latter for spending long hours at the piano. On the contrary, we should think little of any would-be expert who would not make great effort in his particular field.

The same fact should be recognised in the field of religion; for the art of consciousness, on which religious experience depends, is at least as difficult as any other art, and, like any other art, involves training. In the words of Meister Eckhart: 'God is pure good in Himself, therefore will He dwell nowhere but in a pure soul.' But he continues, 'to the pure soul, all creatures are pure to enjoy', for the pure soul cannot be damaged by them, neither will he cling to them. William Blake's well-known lines express the same idea of enjoyment without greed.

> 'He who bends to him a joy
> Doth a winged life destroy;
> But he who kisses the joy as it flies
> Lives in Eternity's sun rise.'

How to get rid of possessiveness and pretentiousness, how to free ourselves from greed, fear, and bitterness, and all other emotional stumbling-blocks to the life of the spirit is the task facing religion on its disciplinary side, not because discipline is good in itself, but because as St. John of the Cross pointed out, no light can shine through dirty windows. In psychological terms, this means that we can only have such knowledge of Reality as we have become ready for by getting our forces united in one direction, instead of putting up an appearance of virtue that is largely meretricious.

The fledgling wants quick and complete answers to his questions about life, but such answers are only to be had for the winning, not for the asking. The question, 'Is there a God or isn't there?' can only be answered by the individual himself through his own search. Others may tell him what they have found, but if he does not find for himself the knowledge is not his. Spiritual knowledge is contingent on our stage of development. 'God is bound to act as soon as He shall find thee ready', said Eckhart, 'but I tell you that no one can appreciate this birth in the soul without a mighty effort.'

As all great men have said, there is no avoiding effort, but if the goal is seen as desirable, the effort will be gladly undertaken, whether in climbing Mount Everest or the mountains of spiritual achievement. Spinoza reassures us: 'If the Way which, as I have shown, leads hither, seems very difficult, it can nevertheless be found. It must indeed be difficult since it is so seldom discovered: for if salvation lay ready to hand and could be discovered without great labour, how would it be possible that it should be neglected by almost everybody?'

But difficult things are not necessarily painful; they can in fact be pleasurable. And Spinoza's last remark has, in the Latin, an almost joyous ring: '*Omnia praeclura tam difficilia quam rara sun.*' ('All noble things are as difficult as they are rare.') From the little child we can learn how effort can be a good thing of which he does not wish to be deprived. If his heart is in it, he will make strenuous efforts to walk on a narrow plank, climb a high tree, or engage in any other difficult feat that will tax his capacities to their fullest; and he will enjoy the struggle and resent any interference from over-anxious adults who try to make it easier for him.

'That is true enough,' some will reply, but why not leave this difficult way of religion to those with a genius for it? Why pester those of us who are not interested and who prefer to get on with our own particular arts. That sounds reasonable, for although 'Religion, like love, exalts us above the commonplace routine of daily life, and makes us supreme over the world, like love also, it is a little ridiculous to those who are unable to experience it',[5] so why not leave them in peace?

Obviously, religion should not be, and indeed cannot be, forced on anybody: but there are two things to be said. Firstly, while we may choose whether or not we will take up the practice of some art such as music, painting or dancing; we are all embarked, willy-nilly, on the art of living and have to do something about it unless we want our lives to degenerate. Secondly, it is not at all certain that there are any with absolutely no capacity for religious experience. It may well be that everyone, however small his spiritual talent, could, if he wished, realise the mystic experience in some degree, and it is doubtful whether a person who tries to keep his life in tune with eternal verities is or could be totally untouched by the mysteries. When such highly developed individuals repudiate religion, they are generally referring to credal belief, not to religion as such.

To have realised the mystic experience in some degree is not, of course, to be a mystic in the sense that Boehme or Hildegarde or Ruysbroeck were mystics. Life only occasionally produces such individuals with a 'genius for the absolute'. But only occasionally too does it produce a Beethoven or a Shakespeare; yet we can appreciate their work and make our own modest attempts at creative expression in their spheres. In the same way, once we have awakened to the consciousness of a deeper Reality than the world of sense and have allowed this spark of illumination to emerge in our souls, there is no longer an *absolute* distinction between the great mystics and ourselves. In so far as we have ever glimpsed that '*mysterium tremendum*' or 'sense of the holy' of which Otto wrote, that 'experience of sacredness which is sui generis'[6] we are of their company, and can follow the Way at our own pace. The impossible is not expected of us; only the maximum that we, at our individual level, are capable of achieving. But any function left unexercised tends to atrophy, and we are warned that 'the atrophy of the sense of the holy and of the moral sense reveals itself as harmful as the atrophy of the intelligence'.[7]

If religion concerns us at all, it concerns us on every front. Every facet of our being, the cognitive, affective and conative, the knowing, feeling and willing, are all involved. We have spoken of the two latter, of mystic experience and of the conative urge to bring our instinctive selves under better control so as to be worthy of that experience. What of the cognitive aspect? The approach to religion for the scientific doubter of to-day must be intellectually respectable, and yet we are faced by the fact that 'God' or the supernatural cannot be found through the intellect. There is no line of reasoning that leads to God save from a major premiss on which not all men, not even all philosophers, are agreed. Therefore the agnostic very reasonably abides by the non-committal attitude of 'I do not know'.

Yet it is possible to take up a more positive and specific attitude towards life, and one which is not unacceptable to the intellect. For just as the defeatist finds plenty of data to support his contention that life is meaningless, 'a tale told by an idiot', 'a discreditable episode on one of the minor planets', so the religious man takes his stand on, and tries to live his life in accordance with, the opposite hypothesis: that life has meaning and that its meaning will steadily unfold and illumine those who follow what Buddha called the Eightfold Path, and the Psalmist called the path of the righteous. It is a matter of choice. To the religious mind, Dean Inge seems wholly right when he defines religion as 'the resolution to stand or fall by the nobler hypothesis' (an infinitely more positive and comprehensive statement than Matthew Arnold's 'Morality tinged with emotion').

What determines the choice between the negative and the positive hypothesis about life, since there is no incontrovertible proof for either? (The atheist may be as dogmatic about his position as the believer, but it is equally unscientific. He cannot prove a negative.) The difference of choice will lie partly in temperament, but also in many other unknown factors. The poet Kahil Gibran described the way in which different temperaments look at life in the parable of the two fish, one of which had a strong 'hunch' that the life they knew under the water was not the whole of life, but that above the sea in which they swam was another 'sea' with different creatures swimming in it. His realistic companion rebuked him for his foolish flights of fancy, pointing to the obvious fact that everything which left the water died speedily. The discussion seemed closed, as it seems closed when a materialist points out with finality that we know no case of a mind existing without a body, therefore such a thing could not be.

Actually, it is no longer true that we have no proof at all of the supernatural. The findings of the Society for Physical Research are sufficiently impressive to cause any fair-minded scientist who studies them to admit the possibility, or even the probability, of other modes of being. But the rigidly orthodox scientist tends, like his counterpart in theology, to close his mind to anything unusual and not already proven by authority, especially to anything which is associated with trickery and sensationalism, as unfortunately so much mediumship has been. Many people therefore refuse to look at the evidence, and denounce it unheard. Such an attitude is not an example of the scientific spirit at its best; neither is it very polite to those careful and exact scientific workers who have produced the evidence.[8] Scientific accuracy and love of truth is something to be highly prized, but bigotry is no more attractive in science than anywhere else and the realm of the possible is very much greater than some scientists seem willing or able to envisage. To Sir Isaac Newton we seemed like children playing with pebbles on the beach while the great ocean of truth stretches far beyond our sight. That picture can act as a stimulus or a depressant according to our temperament. But to many who have sought without prejudice to co-operate with the 'nobler hypothesis', enlarge their understanding of life's processes, deepen their insight into its laws, and keep alive their appreciation of its wonder, to these the evidence has seemed overwhelming that this is a 'Living Universe', and that it expresses more than can be described in strictly causative and mechanistic terms.

To-day we are not so sure as we once were of being the last word in creation. We glimpse the possibility of other worlds and, shocking thought to our egos, other beings perhaps more advanced than ourselves. And if such flights of fancy sound too much like the imaginative fish, we can at least say this: that our inability to live at peace is driving home to us what very rudimentary creatures we are in the art of living. It behoves us therefore to be more humble about our cleverness, which seems able to do so little to diminish hate and cruelty and fear.

Perhaps what is needed is that science should enlarge its frame of reference and start to consider the 'more things in heaven and earth' which it has not yet taken into its purview, rather than that religion should feel inferior because it is not amendable to what is normally regarded as scientific proof.

Religion means undertaking the task of living, not with the crutch of a compensatory phantasy that 'God's in His heaven' and that some day we can go there too, but with the hypothesis and in the faith that, in spite of weighty appearances to the contrary, life does have meaning and needs our co-operation in the realisation of that meaning. If we feel with any serious degree of conviction that this is so, then we also feel that to turn our backs on the conviction would be the supreme disloyalty.

The strength of the faith in 'the nobler hypothesis' varies from one individual to another. It may be nothing but a vague willingness to entertain the idea that 'possibly there is something in what you say' up to 'It could be so; I rather think; I'm pretty sure; I believe; I am profoundly convinced'. It is important to recognise these gradations of faith, for some people seem to feel that if they do not completely believe, they must completely disbelieve or have no opinion at all. They feel it is dishonest not to be wholeheartedly on one side or the other. But if the religious life is one of growth such differences are inevitable; and even the great saints had their times of dryness and ebbing faith.

For those who decide that there is evidence enough to justify the positive approach, or for those who find life untenable from the negative approach, here is an excellent formulation of what Aldous Huxley calls 'The Minimum Working Hypothesis':

'That there is a Godhead, Ground, Brahman, Clear Light of the Void, which is the unmanifested principle of all manifestations.

'That the Ground is at once transcendent and immanent.

'That it is possible for human beings to love, know and, from virtually to become actually identical with the divine Ground.

'That to achieve this unitive knowledge of the Godhead is the final end and purpose of human existence.

'That there is a Law or Dharma which must be obeyed, a Tao or Way which must be followed, if men are to achieve their final end.

'That the more there is of self, the less there is of the Godhead; and that the Tao is therefore a way of humility and love, the Dharma a living law of . . . self-transcending awareness.'[9]

But for some even this 'Minimum Working Hypothesis' will seem too hypothetical. Is it possible to analyse still further and to express the root of the matter in purely psychological terms which ask nothing from us save the willingness to experiment and the willingness to trust those moments of high experience which reveal an inner Light?

Every mature individual who tries in sincerity to think out his own relation to life finds himself faced with a fundamental choice. The nature of this choice was long ago expressed quite clearly in the dramatic language of the Old Testament: 'See I have set before thee this day life and death and good and evil.' The way of life and good is the way of love, of courage, and of continuous growth in understanding. The way of death and evil is the way of fear, of hate, and of a defeatism which finally extinguishes that creative growing point within us called the soul or the seed of God.

Those who, throughout the ages, have chosen and have tried faithfully to follow the way of life have found that it is not a blind alley, but a Path of Attainment which brings about gradual changes within the personal consciousness and an increased awareness of the realm of the supersensory. Consequent on these inner changes and the unfolding of new meanings that accompany them, the conviction deepens that spiritual law is inherent in the nature of reality, and that therefore death is not an end, but a form of birth that sets our spirits free for a larger life.

NOTES

Introduction

1. Cyril Garbett, *In an Age of Revolution*, p. 41. Hodder and Stoughton.
2. A. N. Whitehead, *Adventure in Ideas*, p. 205. C.U.P.
3. Alexis Carrel, *Prayer*, p. 15. Hodder and Stoughton.
4. Sir Edward Marsh, *A Number of People*, p. 25. Harper & Bros., New York.
5. Phyllis Bottome, *Search for a Soul*, p. 93. Faber and Faber.
6. Llewellyn, *How Green was my Valley*. Michael Joseph.
7. Marsh, *op. cit.*
8. Christopher Isherwood, *Vedanta and the West*. Vedanta Society, Hollywood. (Vedanta is a system of philosophy based upon the Vedas, the most ancient sacred literature of the Hindus, and on the Upanishads. The Atman denotes God within, as distinct from Brahman or God transcendent.)
9. Priscilla Robertson, *Harpers Magazine*, December, 1952.
10. Proal, *L'education et le Suicide des Enfants*, p. 127.
11. Beatrice Webb, *New Statesman and Nation*. By permission of the Editor.

Chapter I

1. Aldous Huxley, *The Devils of Loudun*, p. 190. Chatto and Windus.
2. Cyril Garbett, *In an Age of Revolution*.
3. Carl Jung, *Modern Man in Search of a Soul*, p. 224. Routledge and Kegan Paul.
4. *Op. cit.*, p. 264.
5. Paul Tillich, *The Courage to Be*. Yale University Press, Conn.
6. Francis Thompson, *The Mistress of Vision*.
7. Anton Boisen, *The Exploration of the Inner World*, p. 247. Harper & Bros., New York.

Chapter II

1. Albert Schweitzer, *An Anthology*, edited by Charles R. Joy, p. 93. Harper & Bros., New York.
2. See my note on p. 236.
3. Gilbert Murray from Peake's *Commentary on the Bible*, p. 632.
4. Carl Jung, *Modern Man in Search of a Soul*, p. 277. Routledge and Kegan Paul.
5. Eckhart.
6. G. H. Mees, *The Book of Signs*, p. 45. N. Klewer, Deventer, Netherlands.

7. In the ritual festivals of ancient Greece, the bull was one of the symbols of fertility, of new life and power. He was sacrificed in order that, by eating his flesh and drinking his blood, the people might have that strength and fertility in themselves. Therefore the bull was regarded as holy, the Sanctifier, because he gave his life in order that others might live by it.

The Church Prayer Book uses similar language and concepts with reference to 'the Lamb slain from the foundation of the world', and it has not always made clear that such language is metaphorical. Indeed, the dispute over the doctrine of Transubstantiation was concerned with whether or not the bread and wine were *in fact* transformed into the actual body and blood of Christ.

8. Edgar Mittelholzer, *Shadows Move Among Them*, p. 139.

9. Stewart Edward White, *The Unobstructed Universe*.

10. Evelyn Underhill, *Corpus Christi*. O.U.P.

11. Gilbert Murray, *Myths and Ethics*. Pantheon Books.

12. Macneile Dixon, *The Human Situation*, p. 65. Arnold.

13. Aldous Huxley, *Perennial Philosophy*, p. 271. Harper & Bros., New York.

Chapter III

1. Bertrand Russell, *Social Life*. Allen and Unwin. *The Impact of Science on Society*. Simon & Schuster, New York.

2. Anonymous author of *The Cloud of Unknowing*.

3. Whitehead, *Adventures in Ideas*, p. 344. C.U.P.

Chapter IV

1. Margaret Ribble, *The Rights of Infants*, pp. 4–7. Columbia Univ. Press.

2. Ian Suttie, *The Origins of Love and Hate*, p. 87. Routledge and Kegan Paul.

3. *Ibid.*, p. 86.

4. Newton Dillaway, *The Lesson of Okinawa*, p. 14. The Montrose Press, Mass.

5. Gorer and Rickman, *The People of Great Russia*, pp. 97–9. Cresset Press.

6. *Ibid.*

Chapter V

1. Freya Stark, *Perseus in the Wind*, p. 40. John Murray.

2. Frances Cornford.

3. Aldous Huxley, *Perennial Philosophy*, p. 183. Harper & Bros., New York.

4. Sophia Fahs, *When is a Child's Religion Emotionally Healthy?*

5. Mary Austin, *Experiences Facing Death*, p. 24. Bobbs-Merrill & Co., New York.

6. Chaucer.

7. Mary Webb, *Precious Bane*.

8. Richard Herz, *Man on a Rock*, p. 52. Univ. of Carolina Press.

9. Whitehead, *Adventures in Ideas*, p. 342. C.U.P.

10. Niebuhr, *Beyond Tragedy*, p. 306. Nisbet.

Chapter VI

1. Elspeth Davison, *My Child's Life and Mine*, p. 25. Allen and Unwin.
2. Whitehead, *Adventures in Ideas*, p. 368. C.U.P.
3. James Rhoades, 'Out of the Silence'. John Lane The Bodley Head Ltd.
4. *Ibid.*
5. G. Lowes Dickenson, *Plato and His Dialogues*, pp. 15–16. Allen and Unwin.
6. G. K. Chesterton, *Ballad of White Horse*.

Chapter VII

1. Laurence Housman, *Victoria Regina*.
2. Hamilton, *The Mango Tree*. Collins.
3. Walter de la Mare, *The Scarecrow*. Faber and Faber.
4. Elspeth Davison, *My Child's Life and Mine*, pp. 12, 16. Allen and Unwin.
5. Rhine, *Reach of the Mind*. Faber and Faber.
6. Eric Fromm, *Man for Himself*. Rinehart & Co., New York.
7. Phyllis Bottome, *Search for a Soul*. Faber and Faber.
8. *Ibid.*, p. 176.
9. David Starr Jordan, *The Philosophy of Despair*, p. 18.
10. J. B. Philip's translation.
11. Santanyana, 'O World, thou choosest not'.
12. *Meredith's Poems*. Constable.
13. Havelock Ellis, *The Dance of Life*, p. 8. Constable.
14. John Masefield, *The Seekers*.

Chapter VIII

1. Signe Toksvig, 'And did you once?' Short story in *Time and Tide*, February 20th, 1954.
2. Freud, *Civilisation, War and Death*, selections from three works by Sigmund Freud, p. 11. Hogarth Press.
3. Jung, *Modern Man in Search of a Soul*, p. 236.
4. Freud, *op. cit.*
5. From Jowett's translation of the *Symposium*, Jowett and Knight, Vol. I, p. 70.
6. Ashley Montagu, *On Being Human*, p. 101. Henry Schuman, New York.
7. From a poem by Kabir.

Chapter IX

1. Le Comte de Nouy, *Human Destiny*, pp. 89–90. Longmans, Green & Co.
2. W. H. Rivers, *Instinct and the Unconscious*, p. 158.
3. Ernest Jones, *Sigmund Freud*, p. 214. Hogarth Press.

4. Francis Thompson, *In No Strange Land*. Burns, Oates and Washbourne Ltd.

5. Ramakrishna.

6. Jung, *Modern Man*, p. 280.

7. *Rufus Jones Speaks to Our Time*, edited by Harry E. Fosdick. Macmillan & Co.

8. François de Sales.

Chapter X

1. Such studies as *In Search of Maturity*, by Fritz Kunkel; *The Mature Mind*, by Overstreet; *Escape from Freedom*, by Eric Fromm; *The Authoritarian Personality*, by Adorno.

2. Gordon Allport, *The Individual and His Religion*. Macmillan, New York.

3. I owe the remark to Bertrand Russell.

4. 'A Prayer', *Collected Poems of John Drinkwater*. Sidgwick and Jackson Ltd.

5. Le Mesurier, *To my Son*. John Murray Ltd.

Chapter XI

1. Charles Williams, *All Hallows E'en*.

2. Taken from *Time Magazine*, March 16th, 1953.

3. Charles Morgan, *Reflections in a Mirror*, Second Series, p. 54. Macmillan.

4. Wilhelm and Jung, *The Secret of the Golden Flower*, p. 129. Kegan Paul, Trench.

5. Donald Wilson, *My Six Convicts*, pp. 9, 17. Rinehart & Co., New York.

6. *Ibid.*, p. 23.

7. Tagore, *Gitanjali*. Macmillan & Co. Ltd.

8. G. Lowes Dickenson, *After the War*, p. 18.

9. Romain Rolland, *The Life of Ramakrishna*, p. 222. Advaita Ashrama Mayavita, Almora, Humalayana.

10. Arthur Waley, *The Way and Its Power*, pp. 186, 193. Allen and Unwin.

11. *Rufus Jones Speaks to Our Time*, p. 266, edited by Harry Emerson Fosdick. Macmillan & Co., New York.

Chapter XII

1. Aldous Huxley, 'Orion', *The Cicadas and Other Poems*, Harper & Bros., New York.

2. Jung, *Modern Man in Search of a Soul*, p. 223.

3. Anton Boisen, *Exploring the Inner World*. Harper & Bros., New York.

4. Whitehead, *Adventures in Ideas*.

5. Socrates told the Athenians at his trial that he held them in the highest regard, 'but I will obey God rather than you' (*The Apology*).

Chapter XIII

1. James Michener, *The Voice of Asia*, p. 54. Random House, New York.
2. Daniel Cory, 'Santayana's Last Year', *The Atlantic*, April, 1953.
3. Rainer Maria Rilke.
4. Coomeraswamy, *Am I My Brother's Keeper?*, p. 42. Longmans, Toronto, and The John Day Company, New York (Asia Press Series).
5. McCabe, *Henry VIII and His Six Wives*. Heath Cramton.
6. A publication by the White Fathers in the Belgian Congo. Now out of print.
7. Evelyn Underhill, *Introduction to the Songs of Kabir*, translated by Tagore. Macmillan & Co.
8. David Starr Jordan, 'The Church and Modern Thought', *Overland Monthly*, October, 1891, p. 392.
9. Collect for the Second Sunday in Advent.
10. Coomeraswamy, *op. cit.*, p. 50.

Chapter XIV

1. Francis Thompson, *The Hound of Heaven*.
2. James Rhoades, 'O Soul of Mine'. John Lane The Bodley Head Ltd.
3. Francis Thompson, *The Kingdom of God*.
4. Not all drugs have disturbing after-effects or cause a tendency to addiction. See *The Doors of Perception*, by Aldous Huxley (Chatto and Windus), for an account of his experiment with the drug mescalin.
5. Stanley, *Life of Havelock Ellis*. Stanley Paul.
6. Julian Huxley, *Religion without Revelation*, p. 42. Watts.
7. Alexis Carrel, *Prayer*, p. 13. Hodder and Stoughton.
8. Such as Professor and Mrs. Sidgwick, Arthur Balfour and the Verrals, and many others in more recent times.
9. Aldous Huxley, *Vedanta for the Western World*, p. 33. Marcel Rodd Co., Hollywood, 1946.

ACKNOWLEDGEMENTS

I AM INDEBTED TO the following persons for permission to use the items here enumerated:

To Burns, Oates and Washbourne Ltd. for lines from *The Hound of Heaven* and *The Kingdom of God*, by Francis Thompson; Laurence Housman and Jonathan Cape Ltd. for lines from *Happy and Glorious* (*Victoria Regina*), by Laurence Housman; J. M. Dent & Sons Ltd. for lines from 'Corpus Christi' in *Immanence*, by Evelyn Underhill; William Heinemann Ltd. for lines from a poem by Kahil Gibran; John Lane The Bodley Head Ltd. and the Oxford University Press for lines from 'Out of the Silence' and 'O Soul of Mine', by James Rhoades, from *The Oxford Book of Mystical Verse*; Miss D. E. Collins, Methuen & Co. Ltd. and Dodd, Mead & Co., Inc., for three stanzas from *The Ballad of the White Horse*, by G. K. Chesterton; Mrs. Lilian le Mesurier and John Murray Ltd. for the poem 'To my Son', by L. le Mesurier, from *A Book of Verse*; John Masefield and the Society of Authors for four lines from *The Seekers*, by John Masefield; Sidgwick and Jackson Ltd. for 'A Prayer', by John Drinkwater, from his *Collected Poems*, Vol. I.

Harper & Bros., New York, for lines from 'Orion' in the book, *The Cicadas and Other Poems*, by Aldous Huxley; Arthur Waley and George Allen and Unwin for lines from *The Way and Its Power*; Frances Cornford for lines from 'To a Fat Lady seen from the Train'; The Hogarth Press for two lines from a poem by Rainer Maria Rilke; Columbia University Press, New York, for an extract from *The Rights of Infants*, by Margaret Ribble; Pearn Pollinger and Higham Ltd. and the Cresset Press for an extract from *The People of Great Russia*, by Gorer and Rickman; Kingsley Martin for extract from an article in the *New Statesman*, by Beatrice Webb; Constable & Co. for a line from a poem by George Meredith; Macmillan & Co. for a line from *Gitanjali*, by Tagore, for lines from a poem by Kabir, and for a passage from the Introduction to the *Songs of Kabir*, by Evelyn Underhill.

Bobbs-Merrill & Co., New York, for the passage from *Experiences Facing Death*, by Mary Austin (copyright, 1931), used by special permission of the publishers.

I regret having been unable to trace the poem taken from a rhyme sheet on p. 46.